CARL SANDBURG AT THE MOVIES

A Poet in the Silent Era 1920-1927

Edited by
Dale Fetherling
and
Doug Fetherling

The Scarecrow Press, Inc.
Metuchen, N.J., & London
1985

Library of Congress Cataloging in Publication Data

Sandburg, Carl, 1878-1967.
  Carl Sandburg at the movies.

  Bibliography: p.
  Includes index.
  1. Moving-pictures--Reviews. 2. Sandburg, Carl, 1878-
1967--Knowledge--Performing arts--Addresses, essays,
lectures. I. Fetherling, Dale, 1941-   . II. Fether-
ling, Doug, 1947-   . III. Title.
PN1995.S33 1985   791.43'75   84-14068
ISBN 0-8108-1738-1

CONTENTS

iii

FOREWORD

"I am the cinema expert, the critic of the silent cel-
luloid for the Daily News," Carl Sandburg wrote, somewhat
unbelievingly, to a friend in September 1920. The job on
Chicago's most ambitious newspaper had opened up earlier
that month, and seemingly, Sandburg brought no special qual-
ifications to the task. But in the seven years and more than
2,000 films which followed, he took an intense look at the
young medium.

D.W. Griffith, Greta Garbo, Douglas Fairbanks, Sr.,
Lon Chaney, Buster Keaton, Valentino, W.C. Fields--all of
these came under his purview as did such classics as Phan-
tom of the Opera, The Kid, Nanook of the North, and The
Thief of Bagdad. Sandburg thus had a front-row seat on
some of the best years of the silent cinema. He would come
to call Tom Mix his friend, interview a naked Charlie Chap-
lin, and field a reader's query about how many mustard pies
were thrown in a Sennett comedy before a direct· hit was
scored. (The answer, according to his column of June 11,
1925, was ten, as against fifteen pies at the Fox studio.)

Sandburg's poetry collections, his Lincoln biography,
his children's stories, his novel and his folk song books and
other works won him a secure place in American literature.
But in the tangle of his various reputations, his role as a
film critic has until now been overlooked. This book is a
selection of Sandburg's best movie columns plus an examina-
tion of the atmosphere in which they were written.

In a loose, idiomatic and often humorous style, Sand-
burg dealt with short subjects and extravaganzas, romances
and child stars. He commented on props and screenplays
and analyzed title cards and sex symbols. Many of his re-
views and commentaries, written with clarity and color, are

still fresh today. He was not content to merely synopsize
plots as was then the custom with many movie columnists.
The Daily News gave him great freedom, and he used it to
examine films to an extent then uncommon in the daily press.
He was, for instance, one of the first critics to regularly
comment on directorial style. Almost ferociously an advo-
cate of the people, Sandburg warred on the hokum of Holly-
wood, made fun of the trite and the shoddy, and urged a re-
sponsible, realistic brand of filmmaking which would touch
human lives. Some of his recurring themes--for example,
the lack of restraint in commercial features, their level of
violence, and their cost--persist among modern critics.

       The Sandburg found in this book is the Sandburg found
elsewhere only in pieces. In the reviews and commentaries,
the reader will notice the fanciful Sandburg of the children's
stories; the poet with his whims of imagery; the socially con-
scious and committed Sandburg of The Chicago Race Riots
and The People, Yes; the folklorist who believed film could
be a bridge between peoples; and, of course, Sandburg the
biographer and historian dissecting those films--such as
Griffith's--which sought to capture the American spirit.
Above all, the reader will discover Sandburg the pioneer
film critic who brought to the job not only a writer's insight
into plot, dialogue and people but also some concern with
cinematic style and technique. As such, his writings serve
as comment on both Sandburg the man and on the golden age
of the silent movie.

       Our method in presenting the material has been to
provide a mixture of both weekday and weekend feature col-
umns in rough chronological order, correcting wherever pos-
sible slips of the pen and typographical errors in the origi-
nals and using footnotes to throw light on certain Hollywood
careers and 1920's references. When Sandburg returned to
a favorite film or topic, as he often did, we have appended
in many cases his additional thoughts to the main review,
regardless of chronology. We have given our own titles to
the columns rather than retain the stylized newspaper head-
lines, and we have inserted at the beginning of each year's
selection a twin chronology showing developments both in
Sandburg's life and that of the film industry.

       Generous thanks are due Janet Inksetter Fetherling
of Toronto, Maurice C. Greenbaum of New York City, Her-
man Kogan of New Buffalo, Michigan, the Northwestern

University Library of Evanston, Illinois, and Veronica and
Evan Patterson of Loveland, Colorado, for their assistance
in this project.

Eds.

INTRODUCTION

The picture of Carl Sandburg that has come down to us--of the white-haired poet and epic biographer--is not always broad enough to include all of the activities he crammed into his eighty-nine years. The Sandburg persona seems to preclude not only the fact that he was a film critic but that he was a journeyman reporter by trade. Yet it was a reporter's skill, prodigious work habits, and closeness to life that helped shape Sandburg's career. He worked in Chicago journalism in the teens and twenties of the century, the most storied and notorious setting in the history of the American press. It was a time and place in which radical thought and literature melded into one ill-defined but recognizable sensibility. Sandburg came to be considered unique at least partly because he was true to that sensibility while others deserted it and because he remained alive after most others who shared his roots had died.

Sandburg was born in Galesburg, Illinois, in 1878 and later took pride in being the son of a Swedish immigrant who could not write his own name. Young Sandburg quit school in the eighth grade and, with only short excursions into other pursuits, spent the next decade doing odd jobs throughout the Midwest and across the country. The exceptions were brief periods in school and in the army.

After serving in Puerto Rico during the Spanish-American War, he attended Lombard College in Galesburg. There, a friendly professor published his first verse. His attendance at the college was interrupted by his taking examinations for West Point, though he left the Academy after only two weeks. Earlier, in 1894, he had made his first visit to Chicago, the city with which he was to enjoy a long, symbiotic relationship. He did not move there, however,

until April 1906, when he joined the staff of To-morrow mag-
azine, which had accepted some of his poetry and essays.
Later, he called his move "The Chicago Plunge."

From To-morrow, he went to the Lyceumite, a maga-
zine associated with the speakers' bureau that arranged many
of his lectures and poetry readings. But the magazine changed
hands five months later and he was among those who lost
their jobs. In late 1907, Sandburg went to Wisconsin as an
organizer for the Social Democratic party. That position,
too, was short-lived, and he soon came, briefly at least, to
the career that must have seemed inevitable: reporting. He
worked for a time for the Milwaukee Journal and other papers
and served for less than a year as private secretary to Emil
Seidel, Milwaukee's Socialist mayor, before moving on to be-
come city editor of the Social Democratic Herald. But then
in 1912 came a chance to return to Chicago, be a newspaper-
man, and work for the Socialist cause all at once. He was
thirty-four.

Management of Chicago's eight dailies had locked out
the union pressmen, crippling production and circulation. A
radical paper, the Daily Socialist, took advantage of the situ-
ation. It changed its name to the Evening World and reached
a circulation of 60,000. By the time the dispute ended and
bitter competition resumed, Sandburg, whom the World had
brought in as a feature writer, had a foot in the door. He
then moved over to a more stable paper, the Day Book, an
experimental adless tabloid. The staff there included Dan
McGregor, a Scot who was indicted on a trumped-up murder
charge after taking the striking miners' side in Colorado's
1914 Ludlow Massacre. He later fled the country and died
fighting in the Mexican Revolution; Sandburg would eulogize
him in a poem. Except for one brief period with another
magazine, Sandburg stayed with the Day Book until it failed
in 1917. He was, then, laboring at daily reporting when
Chicago Poems was published and he rose to celebrity. So
the pattern was set, not only for his literary career, but for
his double life as both a serious writer and a journalist.

Not long after the Day Book folded, Sandburg joined
the staff of the Chicago Daily News, then the liveliest and
the most innovative and literate daily in the Midwest. The
staff during his tenure there included Ben Hecht (who later
took credit for recruiting Sandburg), Harry Hansen, John
Gunther, Mary Welsh, Robert Casey, Vincent Starrett, Walter
Noble Burns, and many others who would distinguish them-
selves in literature, film and communications.

At the time of Sandburg's arrival, the Daily News also was the focal point of what is now called the Chicago Renaissance. The Middle West was coming to prominence as a cultural influence on the rest of the nation. Such writers and editors as Edgar Lee Masters, Harriet Monroe, Sherwood Anderson, Margaret Anderson, Maxwell Bodenheim, and Hecht were, like Theodore Dreiser a generation earlier, staking out Chicago as their literary territory. They were to make it, in H.L. Mencken's phrase, "the literary capital of the United States."[1] Mencken's claim was much less hyperbolic than that of the Tribune's Col. Robert R. McCormick, who called Chicago "the cinematic culture center of the world."[2] Both pronouncements, however, were at least inspired by truth.

Many of those in the Renaissance movement worked on the Daily News, which took pride in their extracurricular activities and encouraged a certain flair in the news columns. Even those who did not work there congregated at such places as Schlogl's restaurant, a traditional newsman's hangout near the Daily News, or in after-hours cabarets and speakeasies where journalism mixed freely with the arts and the underworld. The atmosphere was such that Meyer Levin, the novelist who followed Hecht as feature writer and at least once substituted for Sandburg as film critic, would recall in his autobiography: "In those days one didn't apply for a newspaper job [on the Daily News] to become a journalist. One applied in order to become an author."[3] Thus, it was natural enough that the Daily News should engage a film critic (then a rarity on newspapers) and that Sandburg, already a literary figure, should be the choice.

It is typical of Sandburg, who contributed to as many fields as any other writer of his time, that newspaper work should have been undertaken in the busiest period of a busy career. His first two years at the Daily News were spent on general reporting assignments. From one such series of assignments came his book The Chicago Race Riots, published in 1919. During his seven years as critic, he published two collections of verse and his Selected Poems, two books of children's stories, and the first two volumes of his life of Lincoln. The biography was researched partly as he traveled the countryside giving combined readings and folk concerts. His concern with folk music in turn produced The American Song Bag in 1927. By the time he left the paper in 1932, after writing a general column for four years, he had published four other varied books and was already receiving honorary doctoral degrees and becoming one of the best-loved

American writers of the time. Even then, journalism was
not wholly behind him. During World War II, for instance,
he turned once more to newspaper writing.

The concept of a newspaper having a critic of films,
free to develop his own ideas and pursue an individual style,
was not unique to the Daily News, though it was uncommon
enough. Only the Daily News, however, would have chosen
someone such as Sandburg at that time. It was a time, as
Ben Hecht would remember, when their editor, Henry Justin
Smith, "saw the paper as a daily novel written by a school
of Balzacs."4

Newspaper reviewing was a lowly profession when
Sandburg entered the field. Most of the major dailies, like
the trade papers, published rehashed plot synopses and re-
written studio publicity. With one or two brief exceptions,
such as Vachel Lindsay's columns in the New Republic in
1915, magazines had not done much better. At best, there
was an overlapping of publicity and reviewing which tended
to blur the distinctions between the two, even at the Daily
News. For example, William K. Hollander, Sandburg's im-
mediate predecessor as critic, left the paper to become a
publicity and advertising man for Balaban & Katz, the Chicago-
based chain of theaters. The historian and one-time Daily
News managing editor Lloyd Lewis had worked for the same
company before joining the paper. Such interaction perhaps
was inevitable in a Chicago to which, as Variety pointed out,
American show business looked for leadership in those days
of posh movie palaces. It was also natural for it to have
happened at the Daily News, which, in turn, took show busi-
ness more seriously than did its fierce competitors.

Melville E. Stone had founded the paper in 1875 and
later brought in Victor E. Lawson to help run it. Lawson
quickly assumed total control when poor health forced Stone's
retirement. He remained publisher into Sandburg's time.
In his hands, the Daily News launched what one survey has
called "a new epoch in journalism in the United States, if
not the world."5 It was remarkable for its innovative foreign
coverage as well as for the famous bylines Lawson accumu-
lated. Those assets, however, have overshadowed its im-
portance in the entertainment field. Its cultural coverage
was a small but important part of the claim by the same
commentator that: 'On a platform of first, last and at all
times the news, without fear or favor, and reliable and de-
pendable service ... The Chicago Daily News represented
something almost brand-new in American journalism."6

No doubt there are several reasons why the paper de-
voted so much space and money to entertainment in general
and to theater and motion pictures in particular.   One is that
Lawson himself was interested in the film industry.   Although
a teetotaler and pious nonsmoker (he also refused to publish
a Sunday paper, a tradition to which the Daily News adhered
until its closure in 1978) he did not take the moralistic view
that movies catered to the public's worst instincts.   Indeed,
during World War I he helped back, and distributed in Chicago,
a French propaganda film, Fighting in France. Another factor
was his determination to give as wide a coverage of various
kinds of news as possible, which naturally extended to news
of the cinema.   A third was the fact that Chicago was close-
ly tied to the entertainment business.   Lawson saw the op-
portunity to make part of his newspaper into what amounted
to a trade paper and a consumer publication for the people,
with the resulting advertising revenue.

There is some reason to believe that the first public
demonstration of the Edison Kinetoscope took place in Chicago
during the world's fair in 1894.   It is also argued that Chicago
was the site, three years later, of the first commercial mo-
tion picture studio.   Whatever the validity of such claims,
there is no doubt that for years Chicago was second only to
New York as a center for films and other mass entertainments.
The legitimate theater flourished, and many plays opened there
before going to New York.   Also, Chicago was the starting
point of several vaudeville circuits.   It has been estimated
that by 1914 as many as 10,000 people involved in the theater
lived in Chicago.

Chicago's first movie studio was the Selig Polyscope
Company.   In 1907 the best-known one, Essanay, began oper-
ation.   The former discovered and made a star of Tom Mix
(whose films were among Sandburg's favorites), and Essanay
at various times employed Ben Turpin, Francis X. Bushman,
William S. Hart, and, for a brief time, Charlie Chaplin.
Emerald, Rothacker, and Argyle were among the other early
Chicago film companies.   At one point, before the austerity
crisis brought on by World War I, there was an all-black
production company there.

In 1910, Chicago producers seem to have invented the
concept of the industrial film.   The city also was home to
the first motion picture trade magazine, the Nickelodeon,
now called Motion Picture Herald.   Even after filmmakers
realized the natural climatic advantages of California, Chicago

remained the country's second largest distribution center.
Also, the giant Hollywood studios frequently would raid the
newspapers, especially the Chicago papers, for personnel--
Hecht is but their most famous catch. Chicago was also the
best place for interviews with actors and other celebrities,
who had to change trains there on transcontinental journeys.
On that as on all other beats, the newspapers battled one
another for stories, displaying a competitiveness for enter-
tainment copy such as elsewhere was limited to crime news.

Sandburg once stated that he enjoyed the critic's job
because he found the cool, dark cinemas conducive to poetic
inspiration. The remark is typical of the self-denigrating
way he publicly characterized himself as a reviewer. It does
not reveal the seriousness with which both he and the news-
paper treated motion pictures.

Devising his own schedule, Sandburg compressed his
viewing into one or two days a week, he then produced six
columns. Each weekday piece was normally a movie review,
plus assorted brief items, such as notes on forthcoming shows,
reports of novels about to be filmed, and such tidbits as the
fact that Lillian Gish's bobbed hair was actually a wig. Sat-
urdays were given over to his features on the industry and
the personalities behind it. The Daily News supplemented
Sandburg's coverage generously. Usually running alongside
his reviews was a syndicated or homegrown gossip columnist
who would complement Sandburg's own observations by noting
what the Talmadge sisters wore and what their favorite color
was. Often there was a column in which readers' questions
about the movies and their stars were answered; another
feature previewed movies which were being filmed.

As well as full vaudeville, drama, recital and concert
coverage, the paper also ran, singly and in serial, many
autobiographical articles by film folk, such as "My Life" by
Mary Pickford and "My Greatest Thrill" by Corinne Griffith.
Perhaps the most popular feature was a "scenario contest"
begun in 1921. It offered $30,000 in prizes and was bally-
hooed by, among others, D.W. Griffith (who wrote a column
giving pointers to contestants), Chaplin and Tom Mix. The
judges included Chaplin, Samuel Goldwyn, Mary Roberts
Rinehart, Gertrude Atherton, and Amy Leslie, the Daily News'
longtime drama critic. The contest was followed by a simi-
lar one for public school students.

Additionally, the paper sent its critics on reporting
trips. Amy Leslie frequently went to Hollywood on such

excursions, and Sandburg made at least one trip to New York and several to Hollywood. In fact, one of his poems, "Without the Cane and the Derby," was inspired by a game of charades at Chaplin's house.

The Daily News and Sandburg were an ideal pairing for that time and place because Sandburg was sincerely interested in the movies. Perhaps it was his concern that kept him from becoming involved in actual film production. Griffith once offered him a consultant's job as a Lincoln authority. Sandburg declined, fearing that despite his advice the film would be historically inaccurate (though he later told others that the fee offered by Griffith was too low). Despite some official proselytizing during World War II, it was not until 1960 that Sandburg went to work in Hollywood, as one of the writers on George Stevens' The Greatest Story Ever Told. Perhaps film, of all the various fields in which Sandburg was involved, was the only one in which he was too much of a critic to be a real participant.

And he was a remarkably good critic considering the rigors of six deadlines a week and the anemic state of film criticism at that time. He enjoyed the freedom of the Daily News and he wrote with vernacular charm and wit, always urging the industry to do better. When it did, and produced an enduring film that would entertain while evoking real life, he returned often to laud the effort. His columns transcended the simple publicity reviews of the time but did not fit into any of the now recognizable currents of criticism. His reviews did look at the quality of films--the authenticity of the sets, the appropriateness of the actors' speech and attire, the caliber of the writing, and, in short, the "how" of the film. Sandburg was, for instance, among the first to recognize the distinctive styles of individual directors. But he also studied the social reality which the films sought to reflect, the correspondence between movies and life--the "what" of the medium. For all that, though, he subscribed to no aesthetic or sociological platform. He was too much of an individualist to be pigeonholed.

At the time of Sandburg's arrival in the field, the principal event in film criticism had been Vachel Lindsay's pioneer study The Art of the Motion Picture, published in 1915. Lindsay had tried to become to film what Ruskin once had been to architecture. He succeeded, at least, in creating a methodology of sorts. He divided cinema into three categories: the action film, which he characterized as

sculpture with motion; the intimate film, or painting with
motion; and the splendor film, or achitecture with motion.
Sandburg (like Robert Sherwood, the other important critic
of Lindsay's time) lacked any such systemization, just as he
lacked Lindsay's knowledge of the fine arts. He had in com-
mon with both Lindsay and Sherwood, however, a literary
background, and he followed his instincts as a writer, with-
out becoming an overtly literary movie critic. As poets,
Lindsay and Sandburg shared a great deal--a relentless popu-
lism and a feeling for common speech. Lindsay saw film as
the only democratic and national art form. Sandburg differed
mainly to the extent that he exercised such a view on individ-
ual films without ever formulating an overview.

As an artist, a midwesterner, a man of modest means
and an erstwhile socialist, Sandburg loathed excess. He
scorned wooden plots and cardboard characters, and decried
the flashiness of De Mille and others like him. Sandburg
wanted the film itself, not a contrived set of title cards, to
tell the story. He yearned for the good, even simple tale,
economically told. "If a base hit will do, why knock a home
run?" he asked in one column. "If a sacrifice bunt is best,
why paste the pill over the fence?"

He was more complex than the language of those ques-
tions would suggest, however. He was a rough man who
had ridden boxcars, for instance, and spent time in jail as
a result. He wanted movies that were well made and sensi-
tive and at the same time realistic and tough. "There is an
idea out in many parts of Hollywood that a popular picture
for the populace can be made if the director stops often
enough and asks himself 'What'll get 'em?' and then answers
his own questions," Sandburg once wrote of a De Mille pic-
ture. "There are formulas. A certain percentage of sex
stuff, another percentage of freak stuff, such as alligators
and skeletons of dinosaurs, and 'swell' people having a
'swell' time so that the garbage wagon drivers the next day
can say 'They have swell swill' .... Classics are out of
the heart and not made by formula."

Sandburg's greatest affinity as a poet was with the
unsung: the fish crier on Maxwell Street, the whore who
wore bells, the Polish brass band. Not surprisingly, then,
he yearned for realism in motion pictures and was pleased
to find "a plain picture about people who figure every day in
the newspapers and the talk on street cars." He was not,
however, an idealist, unaware of the way Hollywood was

skewed. Then as now, money spent was not necessarily ex-
cellence bought. The speed with which 1920's films often
were put together ensured the inconsistencies that Sandburg
found so unreal and jolting. "How long are producers going
to keep giving us plays set in Alaskan scenery where the
roughnecks are elegant and talk and behave like gentlemen
in the centers of metropolitan civilization?" Such clean-
shaven, well-mannered gold hunters, he complained, detract
from the "atmosphere of sincerity" and produce an incongruous
"dapper hero amid the shaggy hills."

Similarly, Sandburg had an interest in good props and
special effects. He marveled in one column at the wind and
rain machines in Griffith's Way Down East. Of another pic-
ture he complained that the director "was satisfied to have
the sky spotted with round stars like Christmas cookies."
The rising sun in that film, he noted, "hesitates and wobbles
like a soft Thanksgiving pie."

Film violence, even in comedies, was another of his
concerns. Slapstick could involve more than mere slapping,
he pointed out. "There is a limit beyond which the audience
does not care to have the large heavy man [picking] up the
slight young man ten or fifteen times, then flinging him for-
ty feet through a barn--and then repeating that identical oper-
ation five or six times within the space of a reel or two of
film." Like the critic of today, Sandburg found himself
wondering whether "it does seem possible to interest movie
audiences for at least a short period of time without having
somebody get killed."

That motion pictures were an industry first and only
secondarily an art was a fact to which Sandburg often alluded.
When he did find a superlative movie, however, he sprang
on it with intensity. The Cabinet of Dr. Caligari, The Cov-
ered Wagon, The Golem, The Kid, The Thief of Bagdad--
he used them all as touchstones. But if there was one "clas-
sic" whose mood and sensibility perfectly matched those of
the reviewer, it was the 1922 film Nanook of the North.
Sandburg called it "a novel and a poem and a biography and
an epic," adding, "It takes the curse off motion pictures to
the extent that those who anathematize the movies without
making an exception of Nanook of the North merely display
their own pathetic ignorance...." The story of Nanook, Nyla,
their children, and their dogs surviving in the Arctic was
the perfect Sandburgian tale. It was rugged and basic; it
embraced struggle and love, and was full of good character-

ization. It was the first successful feature-length documentary, and its authenticity put it a cut above many other 1920's films. The movie underscored the simplicity of Inuit existence and created a respect for their way of life. "It is hard," Sandburg noted in one of his three Nanook reviews, "to think of anything its equal."

The film also had special significance for Sandburg because it was instructive as well as dramatic. He felt strongly about the educational potential of the movies and believed in Edison's prophecy that films would eventually replace books in the schools. In Nanook, he said, it was a "work of genius to throw this informative material into the shape of living, tingling drama."

Similarly, as a journalist, he was greatly interested in newsreels and short subjects. He marveled at close-ups of ninety-year-old John D. Rockefeller, "the emperor of oil," as well as at the sight of fascisti marching by the thousands through Italian streets. "More scenic educational subjects are wanted," he wrote in answer to his own question of what audiences demanded. "The future will prove this. It is portentous that the manufacturers of motion picture machines tell us more of those machines are sold to non-theatrical exhibitors than to theaters."

It would be foolhardy to claim great sophistication for Sandburg as a reviewer, but he did have trustworthy instincts. In 1921, he found The Cabinet of Dr. Caligari a puzzling experience, "a combination of Rube Goldberg, Ben Hecht, Charlie Chaplin and Edgar Allan Poe." And indeed there is about Caligari something almost slapstick, something that could have reminded one of Chaplin and of Goldberg (the cartoonist who specialized in "inventing" ridiculously complicated machines to perform the simplest of tasks). Such techniques were put to use creating the kind of heavy atmosphere of apprehended doom found not only in Poe but in the contemporary work of Hecht, such as Erik Dorn and 1001 Afternoons in Chicago, books much influenced by Hecht's tenure as the Daily News correspondent in Berlin. So although Sandburg did not seem to know the term German expressionism, he showed an innate understanding of what the style was about, and his pen was facile enough to describe it in the crude style of 1920's journalism.

It was a style that suited him, though the haste in which he was forced to work often showed in the finished columns. Even then, however, his humor and colloquial style helped make for easy reading. "Slang," he liked to say, "is language that takes off its coat, spits on its hands, and goes to work." So, not uncommonly, he would "extend a mitt" in congratulations to Griffith or alliteratively laud Chaplin as the "master mummer of the movies," or cite the "p'tickler" heroes in one "melodrammer" or another.

All the while, he remained discriminating enough to resist a number of fads. He disliked the popular films made from Zane Grey novels. He seemed cool to Valentino and indifferent to the coming of the talkies. He despised the common use of gilded endings. For instance, in one 1924 movie a wife seeking reconciliation returns home to her "stony-hearted husband" who, thinking he has discovered a burglar in the dark, shoots her. "Does she come back?" Sandburg asked. "Is the gunshot wound only a slight one so that she recovers in a couple of minutes? Exactly--it's that kind of a movie."

Yet he had soft spots for child stars, animals, comedies and Americana. Little Jackie Coogan was a favorite, especially with Chaplin in The Kid. Coogan "will someday be America's greatest actor," Sandburg approvingly quoted David Belasco as saying. As for Chaplin--he, Harold Lloyd and Buster Keaton were Sandburg's triumvirate of mirth, each with a different allure. "When you leave a Chaplin picture you remember how great he was," Sandburg wrote, "[but] when you leave a Lloyd picture you think how clever the picture was and when you leave a Buster Keaton picture you remember the jokes. In short, Chaplin makes characters, Lloyd makes situations and Keaton makes anecdotes on the screen."

Sandburg was equally fascinated by animal movies, such as documentaries about alligators and the Rin-Tin-Tin dramas. He once wrote an entire column about the "superior, spontaneous, unique, free and easy and natural performers" that are the fish in "animal kingdom pictures." He added: "We may hope and trust that more fish pictures come along in the movies."

More seriously and as befits a Lincoln biographer, Sandburg was especially fond of those motion pictures that sought to convey something of the American experience, such as James Cruze's The Covered Wagon. He saw in that first true epic western, with its vast panoramas of wagon trains,

Indian attacks and buffalo herds, "the nerve and audacity, the pluck and vision" of the pioneers. Nonetheless he disputed the film's authenticity in parts (white-faced Herefords are shown where Sandburg claimed only longhorn cattle existed).   Conversely, he seemed to approve of the fact that, in the Cruze manner, sensationalism was played down. Cruze was clearly a Sandburg favorite for the humor he displayed and for the way he created characters "as real as the people in the telephone book." Another favorite was the Swedish filmmaker Victor Seastrom, "the Griffith of Europe." Sandburg liked his "quiet, telling symbolism and a magnificent gift for making his people human and full of character."

Like modern critics, Sandburg faced the central problem of squaring film's universal appeal with the more exclusive requirements of art. He met the dilemma without fear or favor, as Victor Lawson would have wanted him to, and discovered that, despite the frantic schedule, he enjoyed the reviewing job. It put him close to the people who, clutching their pennies, went to the cinemas and were entertained-- and influenced. Harry Hansen, the Daily News literary editor at the time, wrote of Sandburg: "Theater managers who looked for puffs and publicity could make nothing out of this strange, aloof creature who reported 'movies' in a fashion contrary to all standards of exploitation." Publicity men, he went on, "shook their heads sadly" as the paper rejected attempts to barter more advertising lineage for softer criticism. 7

Sandburg thought movies were important and would become even more so. "Men and women of culture may be aloof, as they please," he noted, "or they may try to look at them patronizingly." But those who do so face the "danger of being in the place of the drum major of the band who marched up a side street while the band went straight along the main stem--without leadership." While steadfastly hopeful on the subject of film, Sandburg seemed to have no illusions about the role of the critic. "So far as the general movie-going public is concerned," he stated, "it doesn't care about [critics'] recommendations." Some of the most favorably reviewed films, he noted, do not generate enough revenue to break even.

"The good critic, the dandy critic," he commented wryly, "is the one whose mind runs with our mind and whose personal taste is like our own." Considered in those terms, Sandburg was a success as a movie critic, and the Daily News

clearly recognized him as such. But the paper's treatment
of his column has led to some uncertainty about the exact
length of Sandburg's tenure, uncertainty which calls for extra
caution in dealing with his reviews historically.

One problem concerns the changing nature of the news-
paper byline. In the 1920's and for years afterward, bylines
were not a reporter's right but an editor's reward, doled out
only for exceptional work or to set off a writer's opinions
from the official policies of the paper. In Sandburg's case,
this means that exact authorship on other than a textual basis
is sometimes difficult to ascertain. Although some sources
indicate that Sandburg took over the critic's column in 1919,
his byline did not appear above a movie review until September
25, 1920. His predecessor, William K. Hollander, wrote the
"Motion Picture News" department until August 1919, and
then for the next twelve months his columns appeared irregu-
larly and in a variety of formats. There is even greater
confusion toward the end of Sandburg's reign, in 1927-28.

It is a reflection of his growing renown that early in
1927 Sandburg began writing a more general column, "From
the Notebook of Carl Sandburg, " while continuing to do the
reviews and movie industry commentary. Subsequently his
byline was used on the movie material only intermittently.
The poet Kenneth Rexroth, who played a tiny role in the
Chicago Renaissance but left the city long before the time in
question, offered a possible explanation. He would contend
that toward the end of his days as a reviewer, Sandburg's
"name appeared as a byline but the copy was written by
ghosts. "8 But this sounds like half-remembered gossip.
The substantiated facts are simply that after the early months
of 1927, the bylines of Sandburg's colleagues appeared from
time to time on the Daily News movie reviews, while for
still other extended periods the film pieces were unsigned.
The byline of Clark Rodenbach, Sandburg's permanent suc-
cessor in the job, first appeared June 25, 1928.

Although several sources suggest that Sandburg's
criticship extended well into 1928, this work shall end with
his 1927 notice of The Jazz Singer. If this seems conserva-
tive, it is also fitting, in view of both the maddening byline
situation and the epochal nature of that, the first successful
talking picture. After all, by his temperament as well as
by circumstances, it was the silent cinema, with its vitality,
fecundity and inherent democracy, in which Sandburg was
most interested; and his reviews, when read as they have

been presented here, constitute virtually a shadow history of the medium.

Notes

1. The Nation (London), April 1920.

2. Waldrop, Frank C. McCormick of Chicago. Englewood Cliffs, N.J.: Prentice-Hall, 1966.

3. In Search. Paris: Authors' Press, 1950.

4. A Child of the Century. New York: Simon & Schuster, 1954.

5. Rogers, Jason. Newspaper Building. New York: Harper & Brothers, 1918.

6. Ibid.

7. Midwest Portraits. New York: Harcourt, Brace and Company, 1923.

8. American Poetry in the Twentieth Century. New York: Herder and Herder, 1971.

See also:

Baxter, John. Sixty Years of Hollywood. New York: A.S. Barnes & Co., 1973.

Everson, William K. American Silent Films. New York: Oxford University Press, 1978.

Jahant, Charles A. "Chicago: Center of the Silent Film Industry," Chicago History, Spring-Summer 1974.

Mitgang, Herbert, ed. The Letters of Carl Sandburg. New York: Harcourt, Brace & World, 1968.

The decade began as one of transition for the cinema and for Sandburg. Rebounding from the war, Hollywood was producing about 700 feature films a year and girding itself for competition from its European rivals. Sandburg, at age forty-two, had rejoined the Daily News, an association that would help make the next dozen years among his most productive. His book of verse, Smoke and Steel, was published, and his first byline as motion picture editor of the newspaper appeared in September. That first column, on a subject to which he would often return, urged moviemakers to aim higher than mere commercial success and seek to produce films of artistic quality.

The bulk of Hollywood's output this year consisted of melodrama, action, and Americana, with stories often taken from earlier novels and plays. Major releases included Dr. Jekyll and Mr. Hyde, Huckleberry Finn, The Last of the Mohicans, and Treasure Island. Although D.W. Griffith's Way Down East--with its famous ice floe chase scene--was a blockbuster this year, the transition from Victorianism to sophistication was under way, a change which Sandburg, in the years ahead, would laud and promote.

Staking His Life

The latest William S. Hart film play, Staking His Life, starts with Bill playing saloonkeeper and gambler, ending with a sign on the front door of the old shebang reading, "This saloon is closed forever. If I can quit gambling, you can quit drinking. Signed, Bud Randall."

In the words of the continuity writer, the play is all
about "how the light of understanding came to Bud Randall
and salvation to Bubbles." The bad woman of the play is
"Bubbles," while the extra bad man is The Horned Toad from
Bitter Creek.

The ingenuity of the theater group surrounding Bill Hart
brings fresh admiration with this film. Haven't they been show-
ing him now for years riding horses, gambling, shooting, get-
ting religion, making sacrifices? And wouldn't we almost
think soon they would run out of fresh plots and fresh air, and
the wild west would go a little stale? Yes, naturally we might
presume just such circumstances. But it would be presump-
tuous on our part.

These studio workers around Bill Hart began to be what
on Dorchester Avenue* they call indefatigable. They either
give new stuff entirely or if they use old stuff they make it
more refreshingly antique.

Take the dance hall scene in Staking His Life. It is
probably the best wild west dance hall scene that has come
along in screen drama. It is from this dance hall crowd
that Bud Randall, played by Bill Hart, picks "Bubbles."

And the Horned Toad from Bitter Creek, he rides into
town, has a shooting match with Bud Randall, aims at a
gambler and kills a minister of the gospel, and rides out of
town pursued by other riders--all as though this was the first
time this p'tickler thing ever was did. Here, as elsewhere,
there are the little touches, the numerous evidence of a
thorough job.

"The coral gates are open wide and the parson's passin'
through," says Bud Randall to his assembled fellow townsmen,
ranchers, cowpunchers and gamblers. He says it with lifted
hand. The familiar awesome hush of melodrama spreads
over the crowd. Closeups of rough men and rough women
show tears down the faces. One wonders what the ghost of
Bret Harte would murmur over the adaptations and extensions
of his ghost stories of so many years ago.

---

*Dorchester Avenue: that is to say, the University of
Chicago.

Bad men and bad women aplenty here. Yet the appeal to persons of reverence who consider religion and morality not only important but essential, is very direct appeal.

The little touches, the numerous evidences of eager craftsmen and thorough workers, is here. They know what is wanted in a Bill Hart play. Here again it's put across. It must be this Bill Hart crowd works outdoors so much. That must be the explanation of why there's never in a William S. Hart play the silly fooling with the darker strands of life and sex sometimes met in films from badly ventilated studios.

The new sweethearts they find for Bill Hart in one play after another shows somebody is on the watch for material of the eternal feminine to match off Bill's eternal masculine. A new skirt for every new play is the working rule here, unchangeable as the laws of the Medes and the Persians.

Staking His Life is showing at the Castle this week.   It is from the W.H. Productions Co.

Oct. 21, 1920

The Testing Block

Fights and thrills and action galore is what you will see in The Testing Block.   There is something doing every minute and some minutes several things.   It is fair to say that "Bill" Hart's latest picture is one of his very best.   But it should have been called "Sierra Bill," instead of The Test-ing Block.

It takes a special caption to explain what The Testing Block means, while it doesn't take any time at all for Bill Hart to show what "Sierra Bill" means.

He's "Sierra Bill" and he's the boss of the "Sierra gang."   He proves it by licking six of his gang in single combat, one after another.   It is a rough and tumble that will live long in the memories of wild west fans, and it is fought for the privilege of carrying off and marrying the queen of a troupe that is touring the Sierras.   Nellie Gray, Eva Novak, is not aware of the colossal scrap pulled off for

her hand until "Sierra Bill, " the victor, torn, half naked and
covered with blood and dirt, bursts into her room at a moun-
tain house in the dead of the night and pulls her out of bed
with one hand, while he covers a J.P. with the gun in his
other hand and makes the frightened official marry him to
the still-more-terrified girl.

Gordon Russell as Ringo makes a swashbuckling villian,
guaranteed to curdle any blood willing to be curdled.   He
beats the pet circus-spotted pinto of "Sierra Bill, " and the
audience squirms in its seats with desire to take a hand with
that quirt.   But he gets him all right.   In the last act the
pony is accorded by its rider,   "Sierra Bill, " the gratification
of stomping all over the prostrate carcass alleged to be the
villain, but probably filled with straw instead of flesh and
blood.   The scenery is of the west wild and it is laid in the
golden days of the golden west.

Dec. 1, 1920

Pearl White

Tiger's Cub, with Pearl White in the leading role, is a
Fox production, directed by Charles Giblyn.   It's a Klondike
picture full of snow, ice, log cabins, mackinaws, gamblers
and much other scenery and character, but always snow in
the foregrounds.   Sometimes the people in this film are not
like real people, but the now background is always the hon-
est snow and convinces.

Drammer, solid melodrammer, is what we have here.
The old theme of a cold, bitter world of struggle and right-
eous people eventually triumphant over the wicked, is devel-
oped.   The girl who ain't got any name except a nickname
of "Cub" given her by her gambler father, Tiger, turns out
to be no legitimate daughter of a gambler at all.   Instead,
she comes from a respectable family--as the plot unfolds.
Likewise, the baby they find in her possession, is--as the
plot unfolds--not her own love child at all, but one which
she rescued because of her good heart.   Pearl White enacts
this role of the heroine in true Pearl White style, and no
Pearl White fan should neglect seeing her in this her latest.

Audiences enjoy this photoplay.   It achieves it purpose
of delivering thrills--not wild and breathtaking thrills, but

good solid melodrama thrills. It does not quite wrench forth tears. But it does lead folks to feel sorry for the character to whom life is cruel and for whom life in the happy end turns out gladness.

Thomas Carrigan is the actor who plays David Summers, newly arrived in the Klondike and immediately flung into a struggle with malefactors for the possession of his father's gold mine and the winning of the heart and hand of the gambler's supposed daughter, Tiger's Cub.

David arrived in the Klondike with a perfect A No. 1 latest model haircut. The barber on the ship bringing him to the Klondike must have cut his hero's hair on the last day aboard ship. Months later, however, as the plot unfolds far in the trackless wilds of Alaska, the hero maintains this same perfect unquestionable haircut.

If Thomas Carrigan again acts the part of a clean sport and a hard guy in the trackless wilds of Alaska, where the thermometer is remorseless and haircuts come high and seldom, we trust he will see that the thatch of his head bears some resemblance to that of one carving his way to fortune and love, in a hard country on the fringe of the primitive; let the roughnecks appear with their necks rough.

Oct. 11, 1920

Film's Educational Value

Dr. G.E. Bailey, professor of geology at the University of California, is working on scenarios of educational subjects, to be made into a series of motion pictures to be shown at schools and colleges.

The value of the celluloid reel and the white screen as a silent teacher, perhaps more efficient than the ablest instructors, is probably only in the beginning.

There are educators who believe that subjects of geography, history, literature, biology, ethnography, anthropology certainly astronomy and some phases of mathematics, can be illuminated and infused with a vitality that will attach fresh power to all that is meant by "popular education."

"I venture to say that if two classes of grammar school children are taught, one by cinema, the other in the usual way, then examined, the screen-taught class would make by far the higher score," says Maurice Tourneur, the French director who is a member of the Associated Producers.

"The screen-taught class would have their brain cells filled with colorful details, while the pupils taught in the ordinary way would have to concentrate to bring up their impressions forced in only by reading.

"Major subjects such as geography, history, literature and so on, can easily be treated by motion pictures for every stage of education.

"Youths and children of all ages will be more deeply interested in a study of the world if they are taken directly to foreign lands, instead of merely reading about them.

"Color the school room with films from Europe, Asia, Africa and Oceania, showing cities, rivers, peoples, how they live, what they do, and you instantly create brain pictures that last indefinitely.

"Cartoon educational films are highly valuable because they show clearly and concisely how things are made. Geology, physics, agriculture, astronomy--all have their highest value in the 'cinema text book.'

"The camera to-day can perform wonders in photography-- telescopic, slow motion and double exposure, with the cartoons--so that any subject requiring visualization can be taught to far better advantage than by book or recitation.

"To-day history is being taught subconsciously by the screen. Literature is another subject receiving indirect attention through entertainment photoplays. Naturally, much depends on the research department of a producer. It must necessarily toil for weeks, months and some cases years, obtaining correct data on dress, custom, architecture and the mannerisms of characters depicting some past period. The result then achieved is pleasing not only to youth and child but to the grownup. It is granted, of course, that the grownup who is truly alive has something of the eager and vivid child soul."

The film portrayals of Pope Benedict XV, now being

shown in the United States, illustrate the point that current history may be made more vivid by the cinema.

Behind the impression of seeing this film lingers a related impression that one has been in the Vatican and stood in the presence of an important personage.

The extent to which traditions are changing is seen in the installation in the Vatican of a projection machine where Pope Benedict personally viewed the film of himself and films of the Knights of Columbus, war employment and educational work.

The extension division of the University of Indiana began last week the circulation of 250,000 feet of educational films over the state, along with 6,000 lantern slides.

Instead of reading thick volumes--sometimes by thick-headed writers--about Africa, the Famous Players-Lasky Corporation alleges that those curious about the dark continent should use films such as those just brought back from the jungles by the Rev. Dr. Leonard John Vandenbergh, missionary and scientist.

Pigmies, natives averaging 4 feet in height, living around Lake Albert Nyanta, are shown on these films.

Twenty years ago Sir Harry Johnson, the British scientist, saw them, wrote about them and tried to bring back to Europe a few of them. They wouldn't come.

They make no protest, however, at showing themselves all over the world through the movies.

Dr. Vandenbergh was accompanied by Dr. George Burbank Shattuck, formerly professor of geology at the Johns Hopkins University. They brought back 36,000 feet of film. And Dr. Vandenbergh, having been nine years a resident among the natives of the Uganda, knew where lay the takes worth taking.

The expedition was financed by the Famous Players-Lasky Corporation and carried approval of the American Museum of Natural History and other scientific bodies. Much data about animals and people contained in the films will be less easily available in the future because of the push of civilization into those interiors.

The pigmies, for instance, are a diminishing tribe, shoved back farther into the Congo jungles all the time by the stronger tribes and by the white man, according to Dr. Vandenbergh.

He notes, too, that as they have grown shorter they have developed a cunning to take the place of stature. Their religion is akin to spiritualism. They talk with the after-world, presumptively, by a mechanism resembling the ouija board.

All of which, taken as straws in the wind, should indicate that the movies are a field of no small reckoning.

Nearly all of the future is ahead of it. Incidentally, the present size of it is gigantic. The total capital invested in all California is $87,000,000, as against upward of $150,000,000 in the motion picture industry in the same state.

Oct. 16, 1920

Sundown Slim

Sundown Slim, with Harry Carey as Slim, will bother some people. This because there are people who like new, ready-to-wear heroes, whereas this film is a hand-me-down.

The play ends with Sundown Slim losing the girl he wanted to marry. This is such a break from the usual very happy fadeout of the Eternal Man and the Eternal Woman clutching each other amidst the shadows, that we must point it out.

Furthermore, we must note that an excellent character portrayal can be achieved by a motion picture actor if the scenario writer gives the actor some kind of an honest chance at a character much worth portraying.

Such a character is Sundown Slim. A sort of good-natured wandering Rip Van Winkle. A "blanket stiff," a wandering sheep herder is Slim. In boxcars, barrooms, at houses by trails, he makes up whimsical rhymed poems for the men folks and the women folks.

Throughout this film the producers gave good co-opera-
tion to Harry Carey in his portrayal of Sundown Slim.   At
two points, however, this co-operation comes far short.

Slim wakes up and stretches himself, listening to the
howling of a coyote and looking at the desert hill and the
starred arch of the night sky.

It would be a great memorable scene--only the photog-
rapher was satisfied to have the sky spotted with round stars
like Christmas cookies.

It looks like a sky of night stars that can be taken
down and put up and scrubbed with scrubbing brushes, sim-
ilar to any ordinary stage place or stage property.

Likewise, the rise of the sun over the desert in the
morning might have been a breathtaking scene.   But the sun
hesitates and wobbles like a soft Thanksgiving pie.

Just a little more care and work on the part of pro-
ducers in this photoplay and they would have achieved a per-
formance possibly equal, in its combination of drama and
leading actor, to the playing of Rip Van Winkle by Joe
Jefferson.

Here's our hand to the producers, however, for the
splendidly American vagabond shown in this play and the
work of Harry Carey as leading man.   It has several lively,
thrilling moments, but mostly its movement is quiet, and
finely, worthily quiet.

Oct. 20, 1920

The Texan

Sometimes a photoplay can be very positively recommend-
ed.   One can say pos-i-tive-ly and with no hesitation or re-
grets, "Go see it."

The Texan with Tom Mix in the leading part at the
Boston is that kind of a play.   It is especially easy to tell
the grown-ups, the fathers and brothers, that this is worth
having the children see.

It's a riding and shooting play, from start to finish, all out of doors. There is a so-so love story. About the only special moral to it is where the hero quits drinking for the sake of the girl he is after.

Oh, yes, we might go along and be p'tickler and pick all kinds of faults in this photodrama. The point is that all its faults are small and amount to little alongside of the big, healthy action to it.

The young folks who want action get it here. The plot is hardly worth telling because it is so much like many other plots. It is the way the plot is worked over into a photoplay. The riding and shooting is heroic, terrifically American, and the desert and mountain backgrounds are superb, nothing less.

The dialogue of the continuity is a little too smart, overdone. But it gets by. Tex, the cowpuncher, played by Tom Mix, has ridden into New Mexico. The barkeep of the first saloon takes away the bottle after Tex pours his drink.

"In Texas when the barkeep removes the bottle I most generally shoots him," is the way Tex speaks.

"Who didn't you stay in Texas?" thereupon asks the barkeep.

"I ran out of barkeeps," replies Tex, whereupon the whisky bottle comes back on the bar.

Later Tex and an Indian find themselves holding money they didn't know was in the saddle.

"That money's tainted," muses Tex; "'Taint mine and 'taint yours."

Nifty--eh wot? Yet continuity writers must live.

"I'll bet you're afraid to go to bed at night because that's where so many people die," is one offering of Tex to a rival.

The New York girl who wanted a primitive hero and has three swift, breathtaking days of shooting and riding in the deserts and mountains, ends with saying to Winthrop, who came on from New York with her, "I'll be satisfied with life on the Erie Canal, Winthrop." And for that one we hand it to the continuity man.

The way Tom Mix always has his hair combed perfect and nice, even after the most reckless bronco riding, is one point where we protest. However, the New York man from day to day gets a heavier beard and appears in one scene shaving himself. In justice to shaves and hair cuts the play is about a standoff.

Every boy looking for clean excitement and the wild life will get a good eyeful here. We all want that kind once in a while.

Nov. 4, 1920

North Wind's Malice

The North Wind's Malice is a photoplay produced by the Goldwyn Corporation, directed by Carl Harbough and Paul Bren. It is a screen version of a story by Rex Beach and is presented at Barbee's Loop Theater.

An interesting and fairly well put on entertainment is supplied by the Alaskan scenery and props in this production. While the mountains, valleys, sled dogs, running streams and waterfalls of our coldest northern territory are the most interesting feature, there is entertainment connected with the plot and the actors who play the play.

It is a long way from the high-notch dramas that have been seen in motion pictures. Yet there is plenty of reason to believe that the reason it falls short is because of speed, speed requisite to the production of the films and subsequent delivery at points of distribution.

How long are producers going to keep on giving us plays set in Alaskan scenery where the roughnecks are elegant and talk and behave like gentlemen in the centers of metropolitan civilization? It seems that far in the wilds of the North where the winds are malicious and life is monotonous, the men use razors, either modern safety or old-fashioned, on their faces every day. Their hair--in this photoplay--is trimmed with the most modish finale of the best barbers in a tropical city. The language of the gold hunters in this particular production is the speech of educated university gentlemen.

Such portraits of character subtract from what atmosphere of sincerity is given to the drama by its many other features.

The plot is fair. The continuity in the opening reels is excellent, rarely excellent in its characterization of the wind in the north country as whimsical and malicious.

The North Wind's Malice might be rated as "average." It was heralded in a way to pique curiosity. The title had lure and a hint of poetry. The mountains, sled dogs, valleys and running waters of Alaska are up to all expectations. But producers and actors come short of anything more than ordinary portrayals of characters and action.

The big high spot of the play is masterly. It is worth while going to Barbee's just to see the one scene where the mail driver is offered a bonus of $100 if he will break his own record for speed between two wilderness towns. In a whirl of blizzard snows the sled gets caught in a tree, the ax for chopping the tree down gets broken, the dogs cut loose and run away, and the driver, amid the whipping winds, lies down among his blankets--and never returns to his old starting point.

Vera Gordon*, who was virtually the star of Humoresque, makes her first appearance since that production. In this, her second important role, she does interesting work, not quite up to her first triumph, the plot and action perhaps not giving her full scope.

Nov. 18, 1920

Griffith's Way Down East

The D.W. Griffith version of the old American melodrama, Way Down East, was put on last night at Wood's Theater. The plot of the stage play written by Lottie Blair Parker is changed only in a few minor details. The impression while looking at the play is that it is melodrama and the afterimpression again is that it is melodrama.

---

*Gordon (d. 1948) was a Russian-born star of the Yiddish theater later associated with maternal roles on film.

As a story this production has none of the originality
that marked The Birth of a Nation and Intolerance, the high-
spot masterpieces of Griffith hitherto.   In wealth of histori-
cal incident and big handling of life also this production does
not come up to the two former achievements.   In point of
acting, photography and sustained dramatic interest, however,
this is fully up to what Griffith has done before this.   In
short, then, Griffith began by giving us thrilling entertainment
mixed with thought and viewpoint of life that challenged thought,
whereas his aim in Way Down East is solely and merely to
provide thrilling entertainment.   This he does put over.

"I love to come to Chicago with my little plays, " said
Mr. Griffith in a curtain speech called for by the audience
after the production was over.   "In these days of Bolshevism
and of tearing down we need to get back to the old-fashioned
wholesome moralities. "

The story of Way Down East is about a girl who makes
a mistake without knowing it.   That is, she gives herself to
a man after a marriage ceremony.   Afterward she finds out
the marriage ceremony was a fake.   By this time there is
a baby.   The baby dies.   The young mother goes to work on
a farm way down east.   Mischievous gossip follows her.   Her
past is uncovered.   She is driven out of the farmhouse by
the stern head of the household.   A terrible snowstorm is
on and she is turned out into this storm.

The son of the stern old man who turns her out into
the blizzard follows her and saves her life.   In order to
save her life he follows her as she runs out on the ice-broken
Niagara River and finds herself too weak to take the final
plunge.   As she lies in a faint on the edge of a cake of ice
her lover jumps from one floe to another.   Just as the ice
cake is about to take the plunge over the brink of Niagara
her lover gets to her, gathers her in his arms and brings
her to shore, to land.   Whisky, doctors--and life again.
Then they are married.

The part of Anna Moore, the heroine, is taken by
Lillian Gish.   The hero, David Bartlett, is done by Richard
Barthelmess.   Their acting is superb.

The music is superb.   There should be congratulations
for those who matched off the various musical passages that
parallel the action of the play.

The barn dance is too terribly and grandly barney and
dancy. Seldom, if ever, have the American farmers gathered
in so great and gay a haymow affair as is here staged. No
farmers have time or imagination for such splendiferous gay-
ety among the cows and the hay in the wintertime.

The villian, Lennox Sanderson, was done to perfection
by Lowell Sherman. Our mitt is extended to him as a paragon
of deviltry. They hissed the villain.

Dec. 14, 1920

What Way Down East Has

Way Down East has two wind machines, one high, one
low. It has two roaring water machines, one terrible, the
other not so terrible.

And--they wash the screen with ten quarts of milk every
day so the shadowgraph actors can have a milk-white surface
to be thrown on. Direct assurance comes that the milk-can
and the auditing account of the milk bill are available to any
who doubt.

When David, the rescuer, is a quarter mile up from
Niagara Falls the small roaring water machine is used. When
David and the girl in danger are about to tumble over Niagara
on a slab of ice, 'tis then the big terrible roaring water
machine is heard.

Dec. 28, 1920

The Mark of Zorro

Some of the prettiest exhibitions of swordplay seen
since moving pictures first were flashed upon the screen are
given by Douglas Fairbanks in The Mark of Zorro, now be-
ing shown at the Ziegfeld Theater. Doug's latest picture
will be considered by thousands to be his best. It is well
within the conservative bounds of a critic to pronounce The
Mark of Zorro one of his best.

The scene is laid in southern California in the roman-
tic days before we wrested that fair province from Mexico.
Zorro is a sort of Spanish-American Robin Hood. He has
conceived the subtle scheme of putting a stop to the abuses
of a cruel, corrupt governor by punishing all who maltreat the
poor victims.   Upon these miscreants he bestows the mark
of Zorro.   This is a bloody Z, cut with a saber on the face
or forehead of the unlucky underling who attempts to carry
out the governor's cruelties or to do a piece of plundering
on his own hook.

Douglas Fairbanks, of course, is Zorro.   He is also
the son of a wealthy old don who sent him to Spain to be
educated.   To divert any possible suspicion, he pretends
he is an effeminate dandy, much to the disgust of his father,
who bewails the fact that the trip to Spain has turned his
son's blue blood into colorless water.   In his quick transi-
tions from the fire-eating Robin Hood to the sissified son of
a wealthy ranch owner, Fairbanks does some splendid bits
of acting.

Ordered by his father, the old don, to pay his addresses
to the daughter of an old Spanish neighbor, he declares no
girl ever will marry him for his money.   Therefore he pro-
ceeds to earn her contempt as a worthless, cowardly dandy,
while he wins her admiration and love by his bravery and
skillful fighting as Zorro.   The windup is thrilling as a melo-
drama.   Single-handed, Zorro fights the captain of the gover-
nor's soldiers and brands him with the mark of Zorro; he
defies the governor and his troops; he rescues his lady love,
whom the captain was trying to abduct; and backed by his
men, who come up just in the nick of time, he forces the
evil governor to throw down his commission and flee.   Then
Zorro sweeps aside his mask.

Dec. 15, 1920

The Floorwalker

The world's greatest Charlie, the Charlie whose last
name is Chaplin, comes across as strong and comical and
bewildering as ever in The Floorwalker.

Only two reels long is The Floorwalker.   But easier
to remember than many products that run an hour longer.

When the observer looked it over at the Madison Street Theater the older folks were all bubbling and rippling at the high spots of fun.

And away to the front sat some child--at a guess a 6-year-old--a healthy rollicking kid--and this little one kept up a steady stream of laughter--a sort of tickle-me-don't tickle-me laughter.

It was not the giggles nor a forced laughter heard from this child. It was the fun and the glee of bubbling healthy laughter. The audience heard it and was infected, sometimes joining in.

The Floorwalker is as good as the best comedies in which Chaplin has appeared. And there are folks who consider it the most preposterous array of puppet follies he has yet come along in.

Two familiar mechanisms of modern life are employed to make comedy. The bubbling drinking fountain and the department store moving stairway.

All the wrong ways to squirt water up and out of a drinking bubbler are here tried and tested.

All the wrong ways of walking up and climbing down a moving stairway are shown with the famous Chaplin spread feet.

The plot ... six different persons would probably report six different plots. It is a futurist confusion of plots.

Also, if it had been advertised that Rube Goldberg designed the faces, figures and costumes of the players, that allegation would sound plausible.

Charlie Chaplin still stands as the world's greatest Charlie. There are millions of people over the earth who know him and are for him, like a brother and a family relation and a gay uncle.

The master mummer of the movies, and great personal tradition of the art of acting in these times, is what we'll say in a world of too much propaganda and not enough fun.

Dec. 20, 1920

Hollywood was becoming more aware of film as art. The release of the famous German expressionist film The Cabinet of Dr. Caligari and the popularity of the earthy Polish actress Pola Negri in films directed by Ernst Lubitsch, helped further this trend. It became clear that the names of prestigious directors, too, could be box office draws. But, basically, 1921 was a year for stars.

Rudolph Valentino won instant, lasting fame with The Four Horsemen of the Apocalypse. The reaction to his grace and animal magnetism surprised even his own studio; when he appeared in The Sheik this same year, he scored another big success. Others enjoying immense popularity included Richard Barthelmess, Charles Chaplin, Douglas Fairbanks, and Tom Mix.

Chronicling them all in his first full year as a bylined movie critic, Sandburg continued his double life. He traveled to Hollywood where he interviewed Chaplin and·other stars for the newspaper, and he shared with Stephen Vincent Benét the Poetry Society of America's annual book award.

Chaplin's The Kid

The Kid is a photoplay written by Charles Chaplin, directed by Chas. Chaplin. The leading role is taken by Charlie Chaplin. It is released by the First National Production at the Randolph Theater.

Those constant contenders who maintain that Charlie Chaplin is the master mummer of the movies and the world's

greatest actor, either in the silent or the spoken drama, now
have another exhibit to put forward in behalf of their argu-
ment.

After seeing such a large percentage of motion picture
plays derived from books and stage dramas based on this
or that story, as originally conceived for a book to be read
through printed pages, there is a thrill about watching the
masterly work of this cinema production.   From the first
click of the silver reel, the action is essentially movie ac-
tion.   The soul of its dramatic theory is motion pictures.
It is a cinema art, the new "eighth art," clear through to
where the woman who lost her baby gets the baby back, and
Charlie Chaplin, the hobo, and his ragtag kid, find a new
glad home to live in.

Having worked slowly and carefully on this film--tak-
ing a whole year to do a picture in the same time that he
used to do six and eight pictures--Charlie Chaplin shows he
has a wise head.   He is centering on quality rather than
quantity.   It is a habit worth the cultivation of other pro-
ducers.

There is a further thrill in looking at this film.   Con-
sider that it will go to the ends of the earth.   It will be shown
the world over wherever there is a town having a theater
with a projection screen.   There will be foreign translations
into all languages, including the Scandinavian, troubling
Charlie Chaplin and the artist who achieved The Kid with him.
Motion pictures don't have to be translated.   They tell their
own story without the bothersome verbs, nouns and adjectives
of labial speech.   In other words, then, Mr. Chaplin stands
on an art rostrum where he addresses the world.   He speaks
to all the peoples of the earth.   As an artist he is more
consequential in extent of audience than any speaking, sing-
ing, writing or painting artist today.   Therefore, it is all
the more of interest that The Kid is easily the co-equal of
anything Chaplin has done hitherto.   And it may be the de-
cision of many movie fans that this surpasses all his pre-
vious photoplays.

There is a touch of tragedy, a constant note of pathos,
running through The Kid.   It opens with a woman walking
out of a charity hospital with a baby in her arms.   She lays
the baby in a motorcar in front of a rich man's house.   The
motorcar is stolen.   The thieves lay the baby next to an
ashcan in an alley.   Along comes Charlie Chaplin.   He picks

up the baby.   A policeman passes, Charlie is afraid to lay
the kid down.   He takes it home and brings it up.   It's a
smart, snappy, lovable kid, a juvenile counterpart of its
stepfather.

As usual, a crack pugilist bullyrags Charlie and knocks
him around.   And, as usual, Charlie suddenly finds a brick
and gives the thug the blind staggers.   Edna Purviance, as
of yore, does the leading lady.   And the kid is an achieve-
ment in character portrayal by one Jackie Coogan.   We can't
see it otherwise than that the teeming millions of boys in
Charlie Chaplin's audiences will feel a revival of interest in
acting.   This film is going to quicken the ambitions of all
youngsters with the tragedy or comedy streak in their blood.

The Kid is a masterpiece and should satisfy either
those who want knock down and drag out or something the
whole family will enjoy.

Jan. 18, 1921

Randolph Theater management counts 140,000 people as
the number to date who have been to see Charlie Chaplin in
The Kid.

Censorship has decreed that one little scene, where
Charlie shows how expert he is at fastening safety pins and
taking care of babies, must be cut out.

Jan. 19, 1921

Visit with Chaplin

Someday Charlie Chaplin is going to show the world a
drama of serious acting.   The conventional joke to follow
this suggestion is the query, "Is he going to play Hamlet?"
The answer is, "Nix, brother, he is not--not so anybody
notices it--but howsoever, when he does get around to a
production of anything approximating the sadness of the Ham-
let play and a grave digger digging a grave and telling the
spectators it is a grave matter--holding up the skull of a
man and commenting on the jests that once fell from the

lips--when Charlie Chaplin gets around to anything like that
in seriousness--it will be a drama with clutches and high
speed."

For Charlie, I found on visiting him in his unprofes-
sional and confidential moods, is an artist of beautiful and
gentle seriousness. Away back under all the horseplay--the
east-and-west feet, the cane, the derby and the dinky mustache--
is a large heart and a contemplative mind. He knows what he
is doing nearly every minute.

Sometimes he refers to the time he will put before the
world a Chaplin film play without the east-and-west feet, the
cane, the derby, the dinky mustache. Those who have seen
him in his quiet, serious moods understand well that it will
be a drama with punch, drive and terrible brooding pauses
of high moments.

I have seen four or five renowned actors (most of them
admit that they are renowned) play Hamlet, but I have not
seen any player better cast for the high and low spots of the
life of the Prince of Denmark than this little mocker of a
little mummer out at Hollywood, making farces for the world
to laugh at.

Not often is the child joy and play heart of the world
to be found in a man shrewd and aware of the hungers and
dusts of its big streets and back alleys. Yet Chaplin in his
gay moods--and his commonest mood is gayety--is the uni-
versal child.

I have heard children 4 or 5 years old bubble and
ripple with laughter in the course of a Chaplin film. They
answer to the child in him. The Kid is a masterpiece of
expression of love for the child heart--love and understanding.

There is pathos about the rain-beaten dusty walls of the
city street where the scenes of The Kid were filmed. The
walls are still standing about the center of the studio lot.
And the thought comes to a looker on, "These are unique
walls, different from stage play scenery or exposition art
works or any similarly transient creation. These walls and
paving stones have already been seen by millions of people
and will in future years be known to millions more who
shall see The Kid."

The home of Chaplin is on a mountainside overlooking
Hollywood and Los Angeles. In a night of blue air the

city of Los Angeles is indicated by lights that resemble a valley of fireflies.

Charades is a favorite game when there is company in the house. After the Japanese cook and waiters have served "everything there is" the guests go in for pantomimes, sketches, travesties, what they will.

Charlie was paired with a young woman who has done remarkable work in art photography "stills." All lights went out, both in the drawing room where the spectators sat and in the dining room which was the improvised stage.

A door opened. Here was Charlie in a gray shirt, candle in his right hand, lighting his face and throwing shadows about the room. He stepped to a table with a white sheet over it. He drew back the sheet. A woman's head of hair, then a woman's face, appeared. He slipped his hand down under the sheet and drew out his fingers full of pearls of a necklace. He dropped the necklace into his pocket, covered the face and head, picked up the candle and started for the door.

Then came a knocking, louder, lower, a knocking in about the timebeat of the human heartbeat. The man in the gray shirt set down the candle, leaped toward the white sheet, threw back the white sheet, put his fingers at the throat and executed three slow, fierce motions of strangling. Then he started for the door. Again the knocking. Again back, and a repetition of the strangling.

The third time there was no more knocking heard, no more timebeats in the time of the human heartbeat. He paused at the door, listening. He stepped out. The door closed. All was dark.

The guests were glad the lights were thrown on, glad to give their applause to the mocking, smiling, friendly host.

At the dinner Charlie mentioned how he once was riding with Douglas Fairbanks in a cab past some crowded street corner. And one of them said in a voice the passing crowds could not hear: "Ah, you do not know who is passing: it is the marvelous urchin, the little genius of the screen."

The ineffable mockery that Charlie Chaplin can throw into this little sentence is worth hearing. He holds clews to the wisdom and humility of his ways.

Every once in a while, at some proper moment, he would ejaculate, "The marvelous urchin, the little genius of the screen," with an up-and-down slide of the voice on the words, "little genius" and "marvelous urchin."

Fame and pride play tricks with men. Charlie Chaplin is one not caught in the webs and the miasma.

April 16, 1921

Chaplin at Close Range

The first time I saw Charlie Chaplin was at his studio apartment fronting on the big lot where he and his company do most of their work making pictures. He was slipping out of his underclothes. The friend who brought me introduced us. Before starting for his bath the naked, sinewy, frank, unaffected Charlie Chaplin paused for a short interchange of thought about climate, a warm day's work, and how they had done the same thing over and over fifty times that afternoon. Whether his clothes are on or off, the impression is definite that Chaplin is clean physically and has a body that he can make obedient to many kinds of service.

Legs, arms, torso, he can relax or stiffen. He can be nimble as a cat or stolid as a wooden saw horse, all at a moment's notice.

He came out of the bathroom rubbing his back with a rough towel, chuckling over how that afternoon he and another actor had rehearsed one little scene and his vis-à-vis had ejaculated fifty times, "Here is your hat--you must have dropped it." Easy and tireless, always working, that is Chaplin. I asked him if he had read Main Street.

"I have had time to read only one book the last year, that was Knut Hamsun's Hunger" was the reply.

We got into a limousine, the best make of a famous car.

"I got this for the lady." he said. I didn't ask what he meant. Later I was told the car is for his mother.

"I went into the place where they sell the car and asked,
'What's the best one you've got?' They showed me this. I
asked 'How much?' They named the price and I said 'Wrap
it up and send it to my home. '"

He speaks in a low musical voice, sometimes with ter-
rible rapidity and then again slow and stuttering. Always his
voice sets the tempo and atmosphere of the thing he is telling
you about.

"Wrap it up and send it to my home"--this was said
with a mild chuckle as though it is only one of a series of
inconsequential nonsensical stunts we go through with every
day to give life's drab a little color.

"What was this interview or conference between you and
Caruso we heard about a while ago?" he was asked.

"The newspapers arranged it. I was to go to Caruso's
room and see him while he was making up for a performance.
I went. At the door we were met by a man who said some-
thing like, 'Spaghetti muchacho carissima Charlie Chaplin. '
We were passed along from one to another till at last we
got to the door of Caruso's room, where the secretary said
the same thing, or something like what all the others said,
'Spaghetti, muchacho, carissima Charlie Chaplin. '

'The door to Caruso's room opened and we went in.
He was standing in front of the mirror making up. He did
not turn to see whether any one had come in--went ahead
with his face make-up. The scretary repeated for the last
time something like 'Spaghetti, muchacho, carissima Charlie
Chaplin. '

"Caruso turned and said, 'O, you come to see the Charlie
Chaplin of the opera.' And I answered, 'Yes, and you are
shaking hands with the Caruso of the movies. '

'He turned to the mirror and went on with his make-
up. 'Make a lotsa money in the movies--eh?' he asked.
And with two or three formal exhcanges the interview was
over. "

Of course, it is impossible to reproduce any story
Charlie Chaplin tells verbally. He tells more than half the
story with his hands, arms, shoulders--with shrugs, smiles,
solemnities, insinuations, blandishments, sentences alive

with gesture and intonation. As a storyteller for a tremendous audience he delivers his story all with motions and no oral speech. The habit is on him of telling all he can with looks and motions. To meet him and talk with him is to understand better that art of illustrating ordinary talk with an accompaniment of hand and shoulder sign talk.

April 23, 1921

The Cabinet of Dr. Caligari

The most important and the most original photoplay that has come to this city of Chicago the last year is being presented at the Ziegfeld Theater this week in The Cabinet of Dr. Caligari. That is the way some people say it.

The craziest, wildest, shivery movie that has come wriggling across the silversheet of a cinema house. That is the way other people look at it.

It looks like a collaboration of Rube Goldberg, Ben Hecht, Charlie Chaplin and Edgar Allan Poe--a melting pot of the styles and technique of all four.

Are you tired of the same old things done the same old way? Do you wish to see murder and retribution, insanity, somnambulism, grotesque puppetry, scenery solemn and stony, wild as the wildest melodrama and yet as restrained and comic and well manipulated as marionettes? Then it is you for this Caligari and his cabinet.

However, if your sense of humor and your instinct of wonder and your reverence of human mystery is not working well this week then you should stay away from the Ziegfeld because you would go away saying Caligari and his cabinet are sick, morbid, loony.

Recall in yourself before going that Mark Twain is only one of numerous moral philosophers who has declared some streak of insanity runs in each of us.

Only two American motion picture artists have approached the bold handling, the smash and the getaway, the stride and rapidity of this foreign-made film. Those two artists are Charlie Chaplin and D.W. Griffith.

It is a healthy thing for Hollywood, Culver City, Universal City and all other places where movie film is being produced, that this photoplay has come along at this time. It is sure to have healthy hunches and show new possibilities in style and method to our American producers.

This film, The Cabinet of Dr. Caligari, is so bold a work of independent artists going it footloose that one can well understand it might affect audiences just as a sea voyage affects a shipload of passengers. Some have to leave the top decks, unable to stand sight or smell of the sea. Others take the air and the spray, the salt and the chill, and call the trip exhilaration.

There are two murders. They are the creepiest murders this observer has thus far noted in photoplays. Yet the killings are only suggested. They are not told and acted out fully. (No censor could complain in this respect.) As murders they remind one of the darker pages of Shakespeare, of Hamlet, Macbeth, and again of the De Quincey essay on murder as a fine art.

Then a sleepwalker is about to kill a woman. He drops the dagger instead, and carries her away across house roofs, down a street. Oh, this sad sleepwalker and how and why he couldn't help it!

This is one of the few motion picture productions that might make one say, "Here is one Shakespeare would enjoy coming back to have a look at."

However, be cheerful when you go to see this. Or else terribly sad. Its terrors and grotesques will match any sadness you may have and so comfort you. But if you go feeling real cheerful and expecting to be more cheerful, you may feel yourself slipping.

The music is worked out well. The orchestral passages run their tallies of chord and rhythm and silence--they growl or they are elated with the story running on the silversheet.

When it's a crackerjack of a production and the observer feels good about it he mentions the screen as a silversheet. Whereas if it's otherwise he says celluloid. Personally, in this instance, one says silversheet.

In a range of three blocks on Michigan Boulevard this week one may see Ben Ami in legitimate, the exhibition of

the "Introspectives" at the Arts Club, and The Cabinet of Dr.
Caligari at the Ziegfeld. It is quite a week.

Yes, we heard what a couple of people said going out.
One said, "It's the craziest movie I ever went to." The
other one said, "I don't know whether I want this for a steady
diet but it's the best picture I've seen in a long while."

Cubist, futurist, post-impressionist, characterize it by
any name denoting a certain style. It has its elements of
power, knowledge, technique, passion, that make it sure to
have an influence toward more easy-flowing, joyous, original
American movies.

                                               May 12, 1921

This is the second week at the Ziegfeld Theater of The
Cabinet of Dr. Caligari. Two reviewers of motion pictures
were talking about the production the other day.

"The name ought to be changed. If this had come from
Hollywood they would have done just what they did when they
shifted the title of Gertrude Atherton's* photodrama from
Noblesse Oblige to Don't Nag at Your Wife.

"And what would make a better title to interest the
movie-going public?

"Call it 'Who's Loony Now?'"

It does seem as though the audiences who witness the
baffling Dr. Caligari and the sinister, sinewy sleepwalker,
Cesare, divide broadly into three categories.

First are those who say, "What's it all about? It is
interesting but what does it mean? Is it a showing of the
workings of insanity? Or am I loony because I don't get it?"

Then there are those who say, "It is some kind of joke
but just who the joke is on I don't know. Sometimes it is
funny as a comic strip in the newspapers. Then sometimes
it makes mysterious motions like a magician when he is going
to pull a rabbit out of a hat. It is some kind of a puzzle

---

*Atherton (1857-1948) was a romantic novelist and histo-
rian; one of the most popular American writers of the 1920's.

like the old question on the farm, 'Why does a chicken cross
the road?' I am glad I went because I have wanted to see a
different movie and this is so different it's a knockout."

Then there is another and smaller group who say, "It
is art." They did not make this for the public first of all.
A group of designers, players, writers, said to themselves
they would produce a photoplay that would be their own idea
of a first-rate movie. Then if it happened the public later
on liked it they would congratulate the public.

In view of these diverse opinions and outlooks, it might
be maintained there would be commercial justice and theatri-
cal propriety in changing the title from The Cabinet of Dr.
Caligari to the title "Who's Loony Now?"

May 21, 1921

Movies and Money

The production of motion pictures is first of all an in-
dustry and only secondly an art. Also the exhibition of mo-
tion pictures is a business first and an art second.

This is the explanation of why there are so many mo-
tion picture productions that look just like a lot of others we
have seen before.

The businessmen running the industry have millions in-
vested in it. In amount of capital invested it stands fifth
among American industries.

More than 15,000 motion picture theaters receive the
output of the industry and give it exhibition. Also thousands
of theaters in foreign countries depend on the American out-
put for new photoplays.

Suppose a film is worked out, finished, and the director
and his staff are doing what they call "the post-mortem," de-
ciding on the final cut-outs and sub-titles.

An artist might say, "It isn't a finished picture, we
ought to throw it away and do a new one; it's not artistic;
we can't let it go out."

That is the moment for a businessman to step in and
say, "We have spent $200,000--or $400,000--on this picture;

already the bankers are saying we throw too much money at the birds in this business; the exhibitors are calling for new stuff; it may or may not be artistic but this picture goes out next week."

So there are good reasons why it is not strictly correct to speak of a place where they produce motion pictures as a "studio." First of all, it is a manufacturing plant where a supply is created to meet a certain and regular demand. But as a studio where artists envision, sigh, cry, laugh and launch their conceptions of beauty, it is subsidiary to its other status as a factory where the wants of a public which insists on "something new" are catered to by business managers and executives.

The plant where Charlie Chaplin works--and he is the owner of it--is in a class by itself. It is a one-man establishment as strictly as the Ford or Edison plants are one-man affairs.

Here is a case where the artist who plays the leading parts, and writes the continuity, and directs the actors is also the capitalist, the manager, the high business executive.

If Chaplin, the artist, says, "That's no good; throw it out!" it happens that Chaplin, the head businessman of the concern always says, "Yes, yes, that's right; throw it out!" There will be more daring originality, a younger and bolder striking of stride across new fields--bigger and more finely thrilling photoplays--when there are more directors and players established as Charlie Chaplin is.

The present writer talked with a notable director in the plant of the Famous Players-Lasky Company at Hollywood, a man responsible for some big, clean work.

He was asked, "Does it bother you sometimes because you have to work on schedule and have the pictures ready for exhibitors on promised dates?"

He answered, "That is one of the hardest drawbacks; sometime I hope to have enough money laid by so that I can have a studio of my own and not send out anything I can't take some pride in for myself."

And there, in brief, are reasons why sometimes the production of motion picture plants seems to be extra monotonous.

The newsreels, of course, are on a different basis from the photoplays. They show us the new president and the new president's wife, the new ambassador to France and the wife of the new ambassador to France, the latest strongman who lifts five horses on his back and how he eats ice cream to keep strong, and scientists such as Mme. Curie, Steinmetz, and Edison.

"Mightiest of all," one newsreel proclaims itself. "Sees all--knows all," says another. And we let 'em pass because they always bring the breath of some fresh event from many miles away.

June 4, 1921

Tom Mix in Chicago

If Tom Mix had had to enter the movie game via an Edisonesque questionnaire he would still be punching cows-- but nobody would know it but himself and the cows. At least so he opined yesterday during his short stop in Chicago on his way east to the Carpentier-Dempsey battle to which he has been given ringside seats by his old-time friend, Jack Dempsey.

"Back in the old days when a man had to have a college education to be a success," he drawled in true western style as he sped along in a car on his way to give the children of the Haven School the treat of seeing him in person, "I used to be pretty worried about my future. What could a rough brute like me do? You don't have to have any education to be a cow puncher, you know--just be able to swing a rope, be a good judge of distance and be able to guess where the sheriff is going to be before he decides himself.

"I thought I never would be anything but a cow puncher and cows aren't awfully good company as a permanent thing, you know. They get morose at times and don't seem very talkative. But then the movies came along and I quit sighing for a college education.

"Why, according to Edison, I'm 93 percent ignorant. I could only answer one of his questions. That was the one, 'What are prunes?' I knew all about prunes because I ate so

many of them when I was a cow puncher that I got interested
in their origin."

Tom's favorite horse is coming through Chicago today
on his way to New York where he and Tom will perform on
Broadway for some picture which is as yet a secret. After
two days of movie acting, the horse will be sent back west
again and the rest of the picture completed there. Tom Mix
writes his own scenarios and thinks up his stunts, which are
not fakes, as the scars on his face testify. His daredevil
tricks keep the Fox Studio people on the jump because their
efforts to get insurance on Tom have met with no success.
They have to watch him closely so that he doesn't do some-
thing too foolish.

As yet he has told no one why he is taking pictures
with his horse on Broadway and his friends are fearful that
he is planning to make a tour of the elevated roads on horse-
back.

June 22, 1921

So Goes Tom Mix

Tom Mix doesn't care. He says so, sitting in a lobby
of the Fox offices on Wabash Avenue, he said it like this:
"What do I care. They say, 'As an actor he's a good horse-
man.' That don't make any difference to me. I don't care
whether they take me for an actor or a horseman. All I want
is that they come and see my pictures and they're doing just
that."

People were calling him "Mister Mix." The mister
stuff sounds off color.

"Would you tell us what you think about fewer pictures
and making them better?"

"Oh, there are fellows with temperament talking about
that. As for me, I start work every day at 8 in the morn-
ing and go on until after 5 in the afternoon. I've done nine
pictures in one year. Done five this year and expect to make
three or four more."

"Have you ever done a film where you doubled, where
you played yourself and somebody else?"

"No, I've never done any regular doubles.   But some
fellow got to impersonating me out in Los Angeles.   Borrowed
$50 one place and $100 another place, telling the folks he
was Tom Mix.   Went to some Texas towns, to St. Louis
and Washington, playing off he was me.   I got hold of him
and nearly broke his face for him.   He made me lots of
trouble.   That's the only case of doubles I been mixed up
with."

So goes Tom Mix, frank, straightaway, radiating the
human stuff that gives his pictures a cleaner and more whole-
some quality in general than many of the photoplays from the
hands of more sophisticated craftsmen who know more about
art and hokum.

July 8, 1921

Short Subjects

Probably each and every moviegoer among the sixteen
million daily moviegoers of the United States has had the ex-
perience of going to a movie theater and enjoying the features,
the extras, better than the main photoplay.

As photography and for pictorial and art values, the
newsreel and the Prisma stunts at Ascher's Roosevelt Thea-
ter this week are among the best this observer has noted
in recent months.

Fireworks make a wonderful showing in motion pictures.
The flame forms, the contrasts of light and shadow, come
through with a fascination close to that of the reality.

A prizefight with two pugilists punching each other in
the ribs and on the head, this is shown--in fireworks as dis-
played in Chicago on the night of the Fourth of July--Niagara
Falls--in fireworks--and an elephant--again in fireworks--
these are among recent achievements in pyrotechnics.

By all means let us have more fireworks in the movies.
Let any Hollywood director who feels jaded and don't know

what to do with some particular scene, let him fill it with
fireworks.

Prisma shows oriental rug makers, how the wool is
taken off the back of a mountain sheep, is carded, spun on
a distaff, dyed, and then woven into the finished rug.   No-
body gets killed.   No man steals another's wife.   There is
no vamping, no dynamite nor bankers, nor bolsheviki, no
hero nor villian, nor love interest, as such.

All they do is live in the mountains with their sheep--
and make incomparably beautiful rugs.

And as we noticed the audience it interested them.   The
sheep, the men shearing the sheep, the woman spinning and
weaving, the kiddies playing in the green grass; they interest-
ed the audience even if they were making beautiful, durable
rugs instead of shooting, philandering or standing on their
left ears.

In other words, then, it does seem possible to interest
movie audiences for at least a short period of time without
having somebody get killed.

Of course, the answer of some scenario writers is that
the audience would sit up shocked and electrified and general
interest would be heightened and intensified if the rug maker
or the rug maker's wife could be murdered for the sake of
what Hollywood and Norma Talmadge* call "the love interest."

At that Hollywood and Norma may be correct.   Having
won public attention and a large following is a certificate
authorizing the bearer to say what the public wants.

Our only point here is that we saw an audience quietly
and deeply attentive while the silversheet was showing a
mountaineer shearing sheep, his wife carding and spinning
the wool, and then the two of them weaving the wool into a
rare and fine rug.

July 16, 1921

*Talmadge (1893-1957) was a major tragic heroine of si-
lent days who retired in 1930.   With her sisters Natalie (1898-
1969) and Constance (1899-1974), both of whom were comedi-
ennes as well, she was one of "the Talmadge sisters."

The Golem

The Golem is a masterpiece of motion picture drama.
It is a photoplay of colossal proportions. It is so simple in
the story it tells and the characters and situations it devel-
ops that any child who enjoys fairy stories and legends would
enjoy and understand it.

Getting farther beyond its simplicity of appeal, it strikes
home with haunting challenges for those who ask for art, in-
tellectual conceptions, accomplishment of design, and the mas-
terly deliberation of sure artistry.

The Golem is showing at the Orchestra Hall this week.
It is one of those few occasional productions of cinema art
which rebuke the ignorance and shatter the assumptions of
those who like to look down on the movies, who feel that the
other arts have nothing to learn from the silversheet.

The art, the play spirit, the mummery, craft and work-
manship which lie back of the production of The Golem are of
the stuff out of which the future of the movies is to root and
establish a cinema art surpassing that of the present hour.

The producers of The Golem are the same people who
made The Cabinet of Dr. Caligari. Persons who have seen
both productions are already disputing which is the better of
the two. The dispute is conducted after the manner of two
Shakespeareans talking about whether Hamlet or Macbeth
should take first rank.

The story is from an old Jewish legend of The Golem,
a mythic figure to be created first in cold clay and then by
ways known to the secret books of wizards to have the breath
of life blown into him. The king of Bohemia has told the
Jews they shall be banished from the city of Prague. A
wizard of a rabbi takes down his old books and searches out
the secret of making The Golem. He finds it. He shapes
a massive clay giant. He calls up circles and sashes of
flame and by wizardry gets the breath of life into the clay
giant. Then comes one of the most sublime scenes ever
put into motion picture film. The rabbi takes The Golem
to the court of the king of Bohemia. The king and his
women say, "This monster does not interest us. Amuse
us, O Jew."

Then the rabbi calls up a vision of Israel, a slow grand
set of processionals across a panorama of cloud. The jazzed
king and his court ladies laugh as though it's a thing to laugh
at. The walls and the roof of the palace begin to tumble on
their heads. Silken women jump from the windows for safety.
The king calls the rabbi to save him. The rabbi orders The
Golem to stand next to the king. Massive stone pillars smash
down on the shoulders of the giant, who stands mutely and in-
differently doing what he is told.

Later is a time when The Golem refuses to do what he
is told. He sets fire to the ghetto--drags the daughter of
the rabbi from her room, pushes down the gates of the city--
and at the end is defeated by the careless whim of a child
he stoops to hold in his arms for a moment.

The music of the symphony orchestra and the chorus
synchronizes and watches the dulcets and diapasons of the
photodrama.

The Golem is a masterpiece and will stand among the
makers of destiny in cinema art for a good long time.

August 8, 1921

The Three Musketeers

The Douglas Fairbanks interpretation of D'Artagnan,
the hero of The Three Musketeers, is sure to go into the
records as one more successful Doug Fairbanks movie, wheth-
er or not it is to be remembered as a specimen of creative
dramatic work.

The literary people who have read Dumas' novel, The
Three Musketeers, as an instance of the French novel of the
romantic school--as well as the people who read The Three
Musketeers because it is a bully book with a lot of swell
fighting and shooting in it--both will be interested in looking
over the latest offering of the most strenuous and reckless
performer in the films to-day.

And the chances are that the literary people who want
an interpretation with nuances will be disappointed. While
the others, those on the lookout for a bully movie that passes

the time, with plenty of clean fighting, good humor, touches of the comic, these will be more likely to find what they started for.

As a spectacle photodrama that cost a million dollars, The Three Musketeers is not much ahead, if at all, of other million dollar spectacle photodramas which have passed before our eyes in recent months and years.

The scenery in the various sets might have cost a million dollars if they were made of some kinds of material, and then again it wouldn't be quite so much as a million if the materials were something else again. Any contractor could write specifications that would bring the cost up to ten million.

However, leaving aside the point about whether this movie cost a million, a half million or six million, it is the acting, the acrobatics, the antics of Doug Fairbanks that put it over into the clear and keep the audiences rippling.

There are fairly good judges who say it wouldn't make much difference if the scenery had cost only a couple of thousand dollars and dummies had been used instead of supernumeraries, the Douglas Fairbanks crowd wouldn't hold it against him. What they come for is Doug, Doug's ways, tricks and manners.

With all the million-dollar scenery, cast, costumes and so on, we don't get the feeling that we are in France and the regions referred to in the Cohan song, "Over There."

Though the Dumas novel says it all happened in France, and the soldiers are in uniforms made up according to research department figures and drawings of what costumes were in the time of Richelieu, it also happens that Doug Fairbanks is so decisively Doug and nobody else that the audience keeps thinking of Doug instead of D'Artagnan, Mary Pickford instead of the queen of France. Without a doubt, too, there are Doug Fairbanks fans who believe that as a performer he is the full equal of anything D'Artagnan might have been, and if he had lived in France in the time of Richelieu, King Louis XIII, the Duke of Buckingham and Queen Anne of Austria, he would have earned a reputation as a daredevil and a go-getter equal to the leader of the three musketeers made known by Dumas.

The presentation of this exceptionally popular film performance is at the Randolph Theater. It is a production of the Douglas Fairbanks Pictures Corporation. Direction was by Fred Niblo.*

Aug. 30, 1921

Red Courage

The old apothegm goes, "Comparisons are odious." And it may be stretching a point. Yet the point seems to be worth registration that Hoot Gibson, the screen star of the Universal Film Manufacturing company, is more widely known among the populations of the United States, and the world at large, and is a topic of conversation with a wide-flung audience of people far outnumbering that which knows and speaks of De-Wolf Hopper, David Warfield or even (may we go so far?) David Belasco.**

The why and the what of Hoot Gibson tradition is worth looking over. Just now Hoot may be seen in a first-run picture called Red Courage, showing at the Casino Theater. As a movie Red Courage has nothing original by way of plot or features. It is a western, and resembles the hundreds of other westerns made by the Universal Film Manufacturing Company in its years of operation.

Hoot plays the part of a daredevil who gets elected sheriff, rounds up big-name criminals and takes the girl away from the archcriminal.

In the final fadeout Hoot has his left arm around the girl while with his right arm he slowly raises his hat till it is about to cover his own face and that of the girl.

*Niblo (1874-1948) also directed such classic silent films as The Mark of Zorro (1920) and Ben Hur (1927).

**DeWolf Hopper (1858-1935) was so often married that he was sometimes referred to as "the husband of his country." One of his wives was the columnist Hedda Hopper; their son William Hopper (1915-1969) played Paul Drake on the television series Perry Mason. Warfield (1867-1951) had been a Broadway and burlesque star and an early partner of Marcus Lowe, the cinema chain owner. Belasco (1859-1931) was the eccentric writer, actor and producer for whom the Belasco Theater in New York is named.

Just before the two faces are hidden by the hat Hoot Gibson gives a long low wink of the eye conjointly with a knowing smile that widens to a grin.

The Universal organization knows what is wanted by its public. It has found the Hoot Gibson type of movie is called for and the audiences don't care if he repeats any more than the Sarah Bernhardt audiences during her decade of playing cared whether that star repeated her gestures and cadences, whether she cried "Armand, Armand!" the same way the thirtieth year she played it.

The boys reading detective stories behind their geographies in school or under railroad bridges playing hookey, don't care about originality. They want the same detective in the same stunts story after story.

So a certain kind of movie audience doesn't care at all whether the plot or the characters are a contribution to original dramatic production. What is wanted among the Hoot Gibson audiences is a performance from a regular guy who undertakes no particular subtleties, but who, somehow, does get familiar with the everyday tissue of the souls of the movie fans who are for him.

The Universal organization goes right along from month to month having Hoot Gibson make movies, working as steady hours as the conductor on a suburban railway train.

And after the movies are produced they are sent over the world by railroad, steamboat, camel caravans, and dog sled, reaching eventually an audience reckoned in millions.

And a considerable part of that audience is located in the remote mining towns, lumber camps and fishing villages, where Belasco is a myth and Eddie Cantor, Frank Bacon* or other stage lights are only vague names, whereas Hoot Gibson is a regular guy met and known through the vivid medium of the cinema screen.

In Red Courage may be seen a fight between Hoot Gibson and an old-fashioned masked robber of the overland stage. Hoot throws his lariat around the robber and drags him on a horse. Both fighters lose their guns. So they go to it, man to man, with fists. As a sport spectacle the Dempsey-Carpentier fight film is tame alongside of this.

---

*Bacon (1864-1958) was the father of the prolific director Lloyd Bacon (1890-1955), who had once been an actor in Chaplin films.

It seems that Red Courage is aimed to meet several demands. It satisfies those who want to see a fight, horseback riding, shooting and frontier life, those who want a love story, those seeking a theme of theft, crime and detection.

Of course, there is no approach to perfection or elaboration in the way Universal presents this. It would be asking too much that so many things should be wrought out to successful conclusion in one production.

Oct. 8, 1921

Expense v. Quality

The last bulletins arriving from the Universal Film Manufacturing Company estimated the cost of producing the film for Foolish Wives at $1,000,000.

A grapevine from Universal puts the cost at $1,200,000, saying further that under the direction of Erich von Stroheim they have produced 300,000 feet of film which must be cut to 6,000 feet.

This is understood to be a record breaker in amount of film. The final photoplay will represent siftings that gave the director and producers different kinds of headaches.

Picking up the best 6,000 feet of film out of 300,000 means work. In the movie business they call that work "the postmortem," which properly slangs it.

Nevertheless, how about this? Does it mean they are going to get a masterpiece of a winning movie because they took a record-breaking amount of film and because they poured umpty umpteen hundreds of thousands of dollars into it? Not necessarily.

We saw Griffith nearly go broke with his lavish expenditures on Intolerance. And the public didn't care much about it; when it was broken into three separate movies it had as good patronage as when the three were in one.

Way Down East, a cheaply produced and trashy movie compared with Intolerance, has netted another fortune for Griffith. Furthermore, there is the example of Over the

Hill*, a cheaply made movie with no expensive sets or costly stars, yet a record breaker in box office intake.

These contrasting specimens prove fairly well that money may be thrown at the birds with expensive production that gets no box office results, while on the other hand the cheaply produced film may draw the steady, long-run crowds.

Carrying the comparison farther along from the realm of strictly business into the field of aspiring art, we find such instances as Chaplin's The Kid paying its author and producer $800,000 at the first jump.

The box office intake from The Cabinet of Dr. Caligari, produced in Germany at a cost of $16,000, was more than $400,000 in the United States, while the figures are even more favorable, it is reported, on The Golem.

Taking two strictly American examples of great photoplays (there are not so many "great" ones but we can number them on the fingers of our two hands or less) and we find that The Miracle Man ** netted a large fortune for George Lane Tucker and his associates, while Griffith was set way back by Broken Blossoms.

And there we are. Von Stroheim has had a big leeway and has spent the ransom of sixteen Balkan kings on Foolish Wives, and it may or may not be what the public wants.

On the other hand some production being wrought out modestly and at low cost in an out-of-the-way producer's lot may prove to be the surprise The Miracle Man was. It is this element of chance that gives a sporting phase to the movie world. It is seen in the breath and speech of men.

Oct. 15, 1921

The Sheik

In every motion picture play that has come from the

---

*Actually entitled Over the Hill to the Poorhouse (1920) with Mary Carr.

**The Miracle Man (1919) was the film that made a star of Lon Chaney.

directive hands of George Melford of the Famous Players lot
and studio, there have been the signs of care and workman-
ship always, if not art.

Usually, if the plot had a good skeleton of action and
character, Melford hangs something worth looking at on it.

This is so with The Sheik, a movie based on a story
taken from a fast-selling novel now reported to be at the
height of its popularity.

It is said to be the first time that a novel successful
by way of sales reached a screen version at the same hour
that its popularity was at a peak in the bookstore records.

The Sheik is showing at Ascher's Roosevelt Theater in
its first run this week. Rudolph Valentino carries the heavy
role, that of an Arab desert chief.

Through varied storm and calm he seeks the heart of
an English girl. In the finish she is apprised that the sheik
is the son of an English father and a Spanish mother, and
they leave the desert to become husband and wife in London.

The pageantry of horsemen and spears on backgrounds
of white sand and sloping dunes is notable. As a spectacle
photoplay it should easily have high rank.

Nov. 15, 1921

Sound and The Sign of the Rose

How it feels to be looking at a movie and then have the
movie shift all of a sudden into a spoken stage play--and then
have the spoken stage play shoot back into the movie or the
silent motion photograph drama--just how this feeling goes
may be known from the production showing at the Chicago
Theater this week, namely, The Sign of the Rose.

The picture play with George Beban in the leading role,
as it breaks into the spoken drama is interesting as a novel-
ty. It may be doubted, however, whether there is any art
to be developed with a series of shifts from silent to spoken
and spoken back to silent.

If the silent is good stuff and the audience enjoying it
then the break into spoken immediately requires another set
of sense organs, those that hear, and the moviegoer who is
accustomed to hearing Finston's platoons of violinists or Jesse
Crawford's* juggling of the cyclopean pipe organ, has a hard
time to adjust himself on the jump to the register of the voices
of the detective from headquarters, the woman who has lost
her kidnapped child, and the suspected kidnapper as they slip
out of the silent moving pictures and emerge into the spoken
stage at State and Lake. A vague lack of something we get
when our picture play grinds its keel on the beach sand and
we jump into a flivver. Or it is like all of a sudden having
our soup changed to coffee or vice versa. We prefer to fin-
ish whatever bowl or cup of narrative we are engaged on be-
fore proceeding to the next item of diet.

The close-ups of the last scene--rendered in pictures--
where the Italian workman after losing his lone child, selling
his furniture, getting his sea bags ready for the trip back from
New York to Italy, meets at the door his wife whom he thought
lost in a shipwreck at sea--this is high-spot melodrama.

Only hard-hearted and indurated sinners would not feel
like responding to this elemental Gallic thing as here given.
And with the cinema close-up those in the farthest seats in
the last gallery (where this reviewer saw the show) can
glimpse the faces clearly.

They put on a shipwreck in the pictures. It goes over.
It is impressionist. The artists in paint, cartoon and illus-
tration, or the old line stage mechanicians of the Lincoln J.
Carter** school, are backed off the boards.

Dec. 29, 1921

---

*Finston was Joseph Finston (d. 1936), a musical conductor
at Paramount where his brother Nat was music director; he
resigned to produce short subjects. Jesse Crawford (1895-
1962) was known as "the poet of the organ," an instrument he
helped popularize in movie theaters as a result of his own per-
formances in the Balaban & Katz houses in Chicago.

**Carter (1865-1926) was a popular writer of stage mysteries
who, coincidentally or perhaps not, was born on the day of
Abraham Lincoln's assassination.

Both Hollywood the movie capital and Sandburg the movie critic were coming of age.

Rather than simply a geographical location, Hollywood was now becoming synonymous with American film. Its products could boast not only of famous stars and directors but of style, size and beauty. It was also during 1922, following several sex, drug and murder scandals, that the film community set up its own censorship and regulation code.

Meanwhile, Sandburg, who continued to travel to studios to further his filmic knowledge, became more outspoken about movies he abhorred or trends, such as excessive violence, he deplored. He also began to see in films some of the medium's remarkable potential for reaching out and educating people. He did this while publishing Rootabaga Stories, his first book for children, and another poetry volume, Slabs of the Sunburnt West.

Gloria Swanson

Gloria Swanson, once an extra girl, later a successful model for modern bathing suits and now a star with few superiors as a box-office magnet, is somehow not content to be merely the first among gown-wearers. She is not all peacock. There is a great deal of the swooping talon-slashing hen-hawk about her.

Evening gowns, riding habits, kimonos, all the panoramic display of a fashion show fall to her in Her Husband's Trademark, which embarked at the Chicago Theater for this

week. Men in dress suits, in the leather puttees of moun-
tain-toppling engineers, men in the horse-worn chaps of
Mexican bandits, Wall Street captains and Pancho-camaradoes*
all came her way.

There are mahogony-made scoundrel schemes in New
York and bandit raids, hacienda gunfights along the Rio Grande.

Gloria, with her Paris creations awakens in herself, at
length, the hen-hawk and strikes Stuart Holmes**, an honest
screen player of sleek villains, as her husband, a pseudo-
financier using her as a social attraction to draw moneyed
victims into his plans.

When he employs Gloria in an especially glorious sar-
torial get-up to trap a westerner, he goes one step too far
and the result is that on a moonlit Mexican night, with the
guitars rendering "La Paloma" under the hacienda balcony,
Gloria awakens to her husband's deceit and to the worth of
the young miner in the leather puttees.

The timely arrival of Pancho, a bad man very similar
to the one shown on the stage last winter by Holbrook Blinn***,
introduces a boiling fight on the stair with the leather puttees
winning and Stuart Holmes dying.

Miss Swanson is building up within herself, perhaps,
that requisite of emotional actresses, a volcanic temperament.
At cheerful byplay, the kittening of curls and blue eyes, she
is a failure. At the exhibition of beautiful gowns she is hard
to rival on stage or screen. She is becoming mistress of
sultry silken moods. Her sullen, smoldering moments are
her most convincing.

A list of music, spectacle and comedy specialties, fit-
ting this film, have been built up around it by the corps of

---

*A reference to Pancho Villa (1878-1923), the Mexican
revolutionary.

**Holmes (1885-1972) appeared in such films as Tess of
the D'Urbervilles and The Four Horsemen of the Apocalypse
and frequently co-starred with such figures as John Barry-
more and Theda Bara.

***Blinn (1872-1926), though mainly a stage actor, also
directed films.

painters, stage directors, and artists who labor backstage of
the Chicago Theater.

March 7, 1922

Animal Actors

With the events of the last year in the motion picture
industry there have been a number of star players disconnected
from the film world.   Some were stars by exploitation and by
managerial ingenuity chiefly, while others had a degree of in-
genuity chiefly, while others had a degree of thespic genius
and have now passed onto the legitimate stage, where some
of them--Francis X. Bushman, for instance--are attractions
on the spoken stage by reason mostly of their old associations
with the silent drama.

However, in a two-reel comedy showing this week at the
Roxy Theater, one may see Mutts, wherein the players are
all dogs.   The producers announce the players are "Brownie
and a doggone good cast, " Brownie being the star.

The plot necessary for these four-legged players neces-
sarily cannot be involved.   The first scenes are in a cabaret,
where a poodle misbehaves so often that he is thrown out,
comes back in, and is thrown out again.

The place closes at midnight, according to law, and the
proprietor, a fine bred bull terrier, goes home and creeps
into bed and pulls the covers over.   Enter then the poodle
which was thrown out of the cabaret.   He seeks revenge,
just as in the human Hollywood play acting there is revenge.
He sets the house afire.

A dog fire department arrives, a dog fastens the hose
to a fire hydrant and plays it on the burning building.   It is
a hot melodrama.   The final flashes show the fine bred bull
terrier waking from a dream on the straw in front of his cozy
kennel.

The use of animals for speaking and barking parts in the
silent drama, the use of dogs, cats, kittens, elephants, mon-
keys, baboons, chimpanzees, gorillas, snakes--these are pos-
sibly only at a beginning.   The story books and the folklore

of mankind are filled with dramatic action in which the characters and deeds of animals form the weave of the story.

We have seen a living baboon or two doing stunts and we have seen contorting, fantastic animals given us by Tony Sarg and others doing animated cartoons.

They have their eye on the mind of the child and the child mind of the adult--and when in doubt they put in an animal, let it wriggle to pieces and then put it together again.

April 8, 1922

The Loves of Pharaoh

The Loves of Pharaoh is a picture play of stature, skill, intelligence, proportions.

There is genius, research, toil, clothes, architecture, design, masterly and expressive faces--and a large cash outlay--represented in the flickering films of it.

The same Paul Wegener* who played Dr. Caligari in the Cabinet of Dr. Caligari, who also played the rabbi in The Golem, is to be seen here as a vividly magnificent "King of Ethiopia." One Emil Jannings** has the role of Pharaoh; Dagny Servaes*** has the part of one who moves on the chessboard of fate from slave girl to queen of Egypt.

The plot is one of as wide a range as Flaubert's novel, Salammbo. And the picture has much of the stark and sure quality of that famous novel.

In stage settings, in revelations of an ancient art and architecture "whose silences hold many of our ignorances," it is a superb production.

---

*Wegener (1874-1948) also directed The Golem and many other films.

**Jannings (1884-1950) came to Hollywood in the late 1920's and appeared in The Blue Angel.

***Servaes was an Austrian dramatic and musical actress whose career extended into the 1960's.

The sphinxes, the temples, the palaces, the art paraphernalia of an old and almost vanished civilization, is presented with a fidelity probably no other so-called "specialty photoplay" has approached.

Ernst Lubitsch, who directed Passion, Gypsy Blood, and One Arabian Night, handled the megaphone at this picture.

Some will call it the best picture he has directed. Others will say it lacks the heart interest and simplicity of the others.

By way of art it is almost as good as going to the Art Institute or the Field Museum. The Randolph Theater is giving it the first run.

"War? What is a war? I love you," murmurs Pharaoh to a woman he wants at the time war threatens.

We might call that one of the pithiest and keenest subtitles ever written. "War? What is war? I love you."

June 9, 1922

Movies and Imagination

The producers of most motion picture plays nowadays are too scared of putting out pictures "over the head of the public," according to John Barrymore.

Scenes are often cut out because "they wouldn't get that in the west, the middle west or the south."

Applying the point to his own career on the stage, Barrymore says, "If I have not always had uniform success it is not because the plays were above the heads of the audience that come to see them.

"As a matter of fact, any girl in a ten-cent store in a small western town can psyche a movie from seeing a third of it. She has seen so many pictures that she can tell you that Myrtle, in spite of the most insistent, varied and acrobatic inducement, is going to retain her virtue and win over Luke's stern old father with the high hat."

Is it lack of imagination the movies suffer from? Are
stories that ought to go two reels spread out over six?
Barrymore says, "There is relatively no imagination."
William Allen White* puts the case likewise, only not so
softly.

Or is there good reason to the argument of picture pro-
ducers who say not for publication that censorship and fear
of censorship stifle imagination and the creative spirit?

Or is it, after all, the fact that the movies are a bus-
iness, a colossal commercial and industrial enterprise, with
imperative orders to fill every week from theater managers
demanding new pictures?

Or is it that the picture industry is so young, is such
a cub, has been so few years learning?

In the answers to these questions might be found explana-
tions due people who complain of pictures, plots and players
repeating themselves and getting monotonous with action lack-
ing imagination from month to month.

Aug. 15, 1922

Blood and Sand

Blood and Sand, the photoplay version of the Ibañez
novel, having its first run at the Roosevelt Theater this week,
gets by as a starring vehicle for Rudolph Valentino, and a
fair bid as a successor to The Four Horsemen, which as an
Ibañez story it is expected to do.

Valentino, guised forth in velvet and plush garments,
legging hither and yon in silk stockings, assuming the lover
tempted and in dire straits through several reels, sighing,
bullfighting, answering multitudinous applause with a flourish
of his cape, watching two women each with a lover's eye,
and at last dying the death of a hero--the part is one up to

_____
*White (1868-1944) was nationally famous as the editor-
publisher of The Emporia [Kansas] Gazette and as the author
of books championing Midwestern values.

the Valentino tradition as such.   Those who rate Valentino
an actor of high degree rather than a matinee hero first of
all will, after seeing Blood and Sand, continue to give him
a top-notch place, while those who count him a quiet, exotic
personality of appeal rather than a young man of rare gifts
in the art of mummery, will ask to see him in more photo-
plays before conceding he has the smoke of genius on top of
talent and looks.

Lila Lee is seen as the wife of the famous matador
Gallardo (Valentino) and gives a portrayal of the Spanish
gentlewoman.   Nita Naldi* plays Donna Sol, the lure, the
sinning angel of the triangle, who gets the heroic matador
in tow, "gives him the air" and sends him to desperation.

He kills the bulls, the hero does, with his sword, fear-
lessly--and a little woman gently pushes him off the cliffs.

Fred Niblo directed the picture.   June Mathis** made
the very faithful translation of the novel into scenario script.

Aug. 24, 1922

Violence

Sometimes the importance of the uses of violence in a
picture comedy make an audience tired.

We have noticed, for instance, a Century comedy, en-
titled A Hicksville Romeo, where the punching of a slight
young man's face by a large, heavy man is carried on for
so long a time and with such realism that the audience gets
no point to it.

If the large, heavy man had grievously wronged the
slight young man and it should then happen the young man
got the upper hand and beat a tattoo of a dozen jabs on the
large, heavy man's face, that would be the ordinary and
accepted retribution seen often in the picture comedies.

*Naldi (1899-1961), a former Ziefgeld Girl.

**Mathis (1892-1927) also wrote the screenplays The Four
Horsemen of the Apocalypse, Greed and Ben Hur.

Occasionally, however, there are comedies where the
director and players seem to have no idea of where to stop
in the rough stuff.

There is a limit beyond which the audience does not
care to have the large heavy man pick up the slight young
man by "the heels" and after mopping the ground with the
slight young man ten or fifteen times then fling him forty
feet through a barn--and then repeating that identical opera-
tion five or six times within the space of a reel or two of
film.

Can't the directors of these pictures be permitted a
little longer period of time for the "post-mortem" on the
film?

Do they always have to send out a picture after it's
been made, even if they don't like it themselves?

Do they smooth their sleep of nights by comforting them-
selves, feeling the public will laugh at anything if the violence
is only rapid and furious enough, even though the events of
the violence connect with each other by no weave of that con-
sidered, deliberate intelligence that must back decent com-
edy as distinguished from cheap, offhand horseplay?

Can't they understand there are two kinds of slapstick
horseplay fun and there is one kind getting the movies in bad
all the time?

Sept. 2, 1922

Nanook of the North

The Nanook picture showing at Orchestral Hall must be
placed on all-round points among the great motion picture
achievements.

Nothing in books of pictures showing the life of the
Eskimo people, with character, action, love, fighting, philos-
ophy--nothing has surpassed this.   It is hard to think of any-
thing its equal.

Nanook is an Eskimo up in the Hudson Bay country.   He

lives with some three hundred of his tribe scattered over an area of snow, ice and water of about the extent of the land of England.

He is a great and shrewd, wise hunter. We watch him dip down head first into a snowy level where he set a fox trap--and he brings up the white fox--alive.

We see him spear the seal underneath the hole where the seal comes up for air. And the capture of the walrus, weighing two tons, a massive animal, one of a small herd that escaped into the sea--one of them holding the harpoon of Nanook in his insides.

And Nyla. She is the wife of Nanook, carrying the baby in a fur sack on her shoulders, chewing the sealskin leather boots of her husband in the morning to soften them that the mighty hunter may go forth for their food.

We see an igloo, a snow house, built in an hour, and a window pane of ice put in. We note the malamute dogs, the huskies, snarling, running, hauling the family sled.

The photography is first rate, better than ordinary. The English concern that gave us this picture has our thanks. For entertainment as a drama, as well as for the knowledge, instruction and "savvy" of it, it is a great picture.

Sept. 4, 1922

That picture, Nanook of the North, is not merely a picture to learn something from, not only a brilliantly conceived travelogue, with facts of geography and points of science worth attention from all those who are for the Darwinian theory and all who are against it.

Besides showing how people live where there is no land to raise crops or food, no timber to cut wood and build houses, that is, besides geographic facts, Nanook of the North is a story.

It is as clean and big and strong a story as Robinson Crusoe. It is as mysterious, sinister and gripping as Treasure Island. Its characters are fewer than David Copperfield but they are more memorable.

Neither Jack London nor Rudyard Kipling ever did a
story that surpasses Nanook. It is up to the best handling
Jack London ever gave to his proposition, "Man is a creature
of the thermometer." And the love life of Nanook and Nyla
stands comparison for tenderness, struggle and mystic hope
with the weave of passion and motive in Without Benefit of
Clergy.

The story of Robinson Crusoe, however, is probably
the best one to compare the story of Nanook with. The Nanook
film lacks the nice and goody-goody stuff of The Swiss Fam-
ily Robinson. But it does have the dramatic loneliness, the
battling with primitive elements seen in Robinson Crusoe,
and then what Crusoe didn't have, a beautiful wife and a
bunch of children that soften up and light up the sinister
white silences of the Arctic.

Sept. 9, 1922

That photoplay, Nanook of the North, is one of the few
films that has come along the past year which is worth going
to see once, twice, three times and more if you feel like it.

It is a classic that takes its place in the film world
as a sort of parallel of Robinson Crusoe in the book world.

Every child that enjoys books and pictures about travel,
and every grown person who would like to travel, should see
the picture for the way it sweeps one out and away from the
things just around the corner, carrying you to a cold, wild,
white corner of the earth.

The film is the product of the Revillon Frères Cor-
poration. They are a big fur-selling concern with head-
quarters in Paris, France. They have stations and outposts
at several points in the far north where the fur-bearing an-
imals live.

An Englishman who seems to have an Irish name,
Robert Flaherty*, a fellow of the Royal Geographical Soci-

*Flaherty (1884-1951) was in fact an American. At twelve
he began accompanying his father, a mining man, on trips to the
Canadian North. He was an explorer before turning to the film
career that also included such titles as Tabu (1931) and Elephant
Boy (1937).

ety, went up into the Hudson Bay district under auspices of the Revillon Frères Corporation.

The idea of Flaherty was to make a picture that would be a first-rate travel picture--and at the same time tell a story, weave through as a drama. That he has done, thoughtfully, amazingly well.

If there ever was a fellow at the Royal Geographical Society who ought to have a medal and a string of medals heralding his own satisfaction and joy as an artist and a scientist, Flaherty is the man.

Nanook of the North is a novel and a poem and a biography and an epic. It takes the curse off motion pictures to the extent that those who anathemize the movies without making an exception of Nanook of the North thereby display merely their own pathetic ignorance of one picture product that stands comparison with the things of highest excellence produced by other arts.

Nanook is a magnetic and lovable character. His wife, Nyla, and their children, their dogs, their pups, their snow houses, they, too, are magnetic and lovable.

Jack London wrote of the white silence of the north, Nansen, Stefansson, Amundsen, and Shackleton have conveyed to us some of the airs of the region whence the people make no wood nor iron, plant no crops, eat no vegetables or fruit.

But the classic that excels them all in its delivery of the character and atmosphere of that region is Nanook of the North, a movie.

It was work of genius to throw this informative material into the shape of a living, tingling drama. One may hear the children ripple with laughter at various places in this picture play.

Nanook comes in a sealhide canoe. He is landing. He seems to be alone. He goes back to the canoe, dips down into the one big hole in the top of the canoe and brings out his wife, with a fine naked baby in a pouch on the back, goes back again for two husky boys one by one, and last of all the pups they are raising. Of course, the children laugh. It has a magic and surprise.

The final scene shows the family sleeping in a snow

house while outside the wolf dogs howl as the snow piles on
their hair.   We see the winds sweeping long levels of snow.
We flash inside the house and the last of the film is the
sleeping face of Nanook, peaceful, masterly, ready with his
brood around him, ready for anything.

We have seen him trap a live fox and bring the live
fox up out of the snow with his bare hands.   We have seen
him harpoon him a walrus and drag forth a seal from under
the ice.   We have seen him driving his snarling dogs through
a fierce blizzard with his Nyla and the little ones.   It was
a stroke of dramatic art to show him last of all sleeping
with peace and understanding on his face.

Oct. 21, 1922

Newsreels

There are some weeks when the motion picture news-
reels are rich and vivid with impressions of life, people,
events.

The Pathé newsreel, of course, comes a little short of
the claim that it "sees all, knows all." Yet there are weeks
when it brims with a spilling over of life.

The close-ups of John D. Rockefeller attending church
are without doubt the most extraordinary captures made dur-
ing his lifetime of the physical and outward form of the wealth-
iest man in the world.

The emperor of oil steps forth from the church door,
takes several steps along a sidewalk, and then steps into a
movie camera close-up.

It is not a human face for an offhand analysis and de-
piction.   He looks straight into the camera, he smiles, he
twinkles his inscrutable eyes.

It is the face of a man who has made his reconciliations
with any and all things bothering what is called conscience or
disturbing his inward peace.

Furthermore, it is the face of a man whose will, [illegible] and regime have conquered nervous dyspepsia, made an old stomach new, traveling on into ninety years.

There are many thoughts come on gazing into these features of this, the most powerful figure of industry and finance in the world.

Contrast comes with jaunty Lloyd George*, who follows, smiling, hand-shaking, campaigning over Great Britain for a vindication of his governmental policies.

Then the fascisti marching by thousands in the streets of Italian cities, closing with a group in which the face of Mussolini is in the center.

History in the making comes before one's eyes in the work of inventors and the carrying on of experiments.

Thus, while the Pathé camera isn't quite where it "sees all, knows all," it does have a pair of glims that are making valuable records.

Nov. 18, 1922

Robin Hood

The first public showing of Robin Hood, the latest Douglas Fairbanks picture, on which he has been working ten months, came off last night at Cohan's Grand Theater. Fairbanks himself was there, seated with Mary Pickford in a box.

The audience called for speeches. Mary Pickford threw kisses and Doug stood up and made this speech. "I'm so nervous and excited I don't know what to do with myself. I hope you'll like my picture." In an intermission speech of about equal length, he concluded by saying, "If you like the picture I'll be tickled to death."

The story of Robin Hood, the English outlaw, that

_____
*Prime Minister David Lloyd George (1863-1945) whose Liberal government was defeated in the general election of 1922.

legendary character who becomes known to all school children
who read their books, is told in this silversheet rendition
with a skill and a graphic power that will put it across to
any boy or girl [illegible] more vividly and humanly than any
of the story books.   It will be a screen classic very likely.

It is not a child story, simply and merely.   It has punch
and go, a passing of puppets and a grand balance of the comic,
so that it is a picture for grown-ups as well as the kiddies.

The story as given in some versions in the books is
departed from, yet not in any way so as to mar the main
point of the Robin Hood tradition.   The production is giant!
It is evident that a faithful research department worked hard
and the costumes and the builders of sets had a big leeway
in an expense account.

This is Douglas Fairbanks' masterpiece; it will win him
new friends and hold all his old ones.   The outpouring of
people who couldn't get inside the theater, but waited around
for a look at him was probably the largest crowd of its kind
that the local theater district has seen.   It was a testimony
to a unique personal popularity.

Besides Fairbanks' strong work as Robin Hood, there is
the characterization of Richard the Lion-Hearted by Wallace
Beery.   It is exceptionally strong.   Enid Bennett* first ap-
pears as Lady Marian Fitzwalter--and takes her place among
the women of grace in the screen world.

Elton Thomas**, who is responsible for the story, should
be given praise.   To hold a movie audience two hours and
weave all the strands together like a complete novel, is a
task--and here well done.   The direction was by Allan Dwan***,
the photography by Arthur Edeson****, and both are to be con-
gratulated.

_____
*Bennett (1895-1969), a transplanted Australian actress of
the day.

**"Elton Thomas" was in fact a pseudonym of Douglas
Fairbanks, whose real name was Douglas Elton Ullmann.

***Dwan (1885-1981), the prolific Canadian-born director.

****Edeson (1891-1970), a former portrait photographer,
was cinematographer on many Fairbanks films.

Good luck and a long run to the new Douglas Fairbanks picture. It will make new friends and set new standards for the movies.

Charlie Chaplin sent a floral piece, a large target of white roses and carnations, inscribed, "Sure to hit the bull's eye." Of course, Charlie knows what he meant by "bull's eye." The job has its percentage of hokum. But as art goes, its percentage of honesty and sincerity is high.

Oct. 17, 1922

With Hollywood's hegemony established, European film artists began pouring into America. Mary Pickford's importation of Ernst Lubitsch a year earlier suggested American nationalism had receded sufficiently to allow German artists to work. Soon the list of emigrés would include such directors as Michael Curtiz, F.W. Murnau, Victor Seastrom, and Mauritz Stiller (plus his protégé, Greta Garbo). At first there were problems with heavy accents and autocratic methods. But soon European subtlety, sexual sophistication, and visual style had become part of the Hollywood product. Sandburg, unlike some reviewers, did not resist this trend but praised many of the Europeans, especially Seastrom. Perhaps in part due to his training as a poet, Sandburg also argued for economy and discipline in movie scenarios.

Also in 1923, the Rivoli Theatre in New York presented a program of short films with synchronized sound. Interest was slight, and the experiment was not repeated. But the future was clear nonetheless.

Filmless Movies

At a Sunday-night benefit performance recently the newspaper columnist, Franklin P. Adams, offered a stunt he called "A Filmless Movie."

He read off a row of moving picture subtitles. Anyone with a little imagination who knows the movies could just sit back with eyes shut and fill in the picture reels.

This columnist's experiment sort of ties up with a trick

they did at Columbia University, where they have a de-
partment teaching the teachable things of the picture business.
University students were sent to movies with instructions to
copy all the subtitles. They came back with notebooks out of
which anyone--with a little imagination--could have the "film-
less movie" just by reading the notebook of subtitles.

Of course, if this scheme is carried too far and en-
couraged too much, so that our young people learn to work
their own imaginations and run off their own "filmless movies"
from pages of subtitles, there is no telling where it may
end.

It might reach the time when the straphangers on the
street cars will stand up hanging their left hands in leather
and their right hands in pages of subtitles which they will be
reading. Some will be seeing the filmless movies full of
pathetic scenes and they will be crying, letting go of the
strap to take out their handkerchiefs, while others will be
enjoying the comedy filmless movie. And those would be
strange scenes to look at in our rush-hour street cars.

There would be sure to be some people reading the
murder trials, the Ruhr occupation and the market reports
in the newspapers, and they as practical people would feel
sorry for the filmless movie fans, cursed with such handy
imaginations.

The fiction magazines, of course, could use the same
idea for the benefit of their readers who don't have time to
read all the stories. Little thumbnail summaries and sketch-
es of the plots and characters could be published. It would
all fit in with the tabloid trend of the time, tabloid histories
of the world and mankind, tabloid outlines of science, and
so on.

We were just getting serious about this thing when
Lloyd Lewis* came in and when we put up the matter to him,
he said that he can sit in the Chicago Theater and by closing
his eyes and listening to the pipe organ playing of Jesse
Crawford he knows whether the silversheet is flickering off
kisses, tears, fights, funerals or humpty dumpty horseplay.

Mar. 17, 1923

*Lewis was a Chicago writer who, in the period from 1931
to 1945, would be by turns the drama critic, sports editor
and managing editor of the Daily News.

Edison's Prophecy

Edison's idea that films are going to take the place of books in the teaching of children in schools is an idea that will stand up.

Of course, the average sensational hokum sketch, of the type of Cecil De Mille's Male and Female with its punctuations of silk stockings and its rehearsals of the Hollywood fifty-seven varieties of movie kisses--this is not what Edison had in mind.

Edison means pictures like those of H. A. Snow* and of Mr. and Mrs. Martin Johnson**, with their close-ups of elephants, giraffes, zebras, snakes, wart hogs, rhinoceri, hippopotami--the zoo in the wild.

It may be that five or six pictures out of Hollywood the last ten years may be alive and called for by the picture fans ten years from now.

It is a cinch that the African animal pictures, taken at risk of life, and under stress of the hot sun, the jungle fever perils, will be of value among high school and college students for many years to come.

Other pictures from Africa, of a similar type, will come along, some that surpass by far those already made.

Yet those already made have a documentary value. They are testimony of what was at a certain time in certain places.

Entirely aside from their scientific value, their biological, zoological and geographic features, the Snow and the Martin Johnson pictures are something else.

---

*Snow made adventure-nature documentaries such as Lost in the Arctic (1920).

**Martin Johnson and Osa Leighty Johnson circled the globe making and exhibiting such films as Hunting Big Game in Africa; she carried on the work after he died in 1937 when the aircraft in which they were travelling crashed. His life of adventure had begun when he served as cook and photographer aboard Jack London's boat Snark on its voyage to the South Pacific.

They are thrilling adventure stories in the full sense of that word thrilling as applied to "wild tales for boys" or the shocks and surprises of melodrama.

To teach boys facts of scientific worth, letting them understand better the earth and the animals thereof in the dusks and dawns of life, while at the same hour they are having a whacking bully time--this is performance of a task in education.

Edison's prophecy will hold. There is a public just as much interested in the wild animals of Africa as in the wild women offered by Hollywood.

As between Jesse Lasky and Cecil De Mille on what the public wants, and on the other hand Thomas Edison and Will Hays, * the guesses of the two latter would be safer as to what the public wants, in the long run, of movie stuff with nourishment in it.

May 19, 1923

Einstein

One of the best films in Chicago at the present hour is the motion picture explaining Einstein, which is having its first run at McVicker's Theater this week.

The Scientific American a few months ago announced that this picture had been made and that from a technical and educational standpoint, the editors said, it was extraordinary.

Of course we understand a thing might please the editors of the Scientific American and be a fine thing from their way of looking at it--and then not count for very much as a regular picture in a place where they have been showing Gloria Swanson in all her glory or Elliot Dexter**in all his dexterousness.

----

*Hays (1879-1954) had become the first president of the Motion Picture Producers' and Distributors' Association of America in 1922 but did not write its notorious Production Code, or censorship guidelines, until 1930.

**Dexter (1870-1941) was a retired vaudevillian who made several films including Only 38.

However that may be, they did a mighty good job on this Einstein film. They make it clear that Einstein has a grand old skypiece--a high speed think tank--and we get a little look at what is going on inside of the works.

That Einstein and maybe only a dozen men in the world would understand his book on relativity ought not to scare anybody away from the picture.

There is a lot of entertainment in it--maybe a little laugh or smile here and there.

Of course, the boys and girls who are out to be "stepping high" or those who must have a story with a plot and somebody getting killed or falling in love or falling into a pile of money or falling down a coal hole--well, they won't get so very much out of this film--they will have to pass it up and try something else, such as Only 38*, the main feature film on the same program at McVicker's.

But there are people who will enjoy this Einstein picture, because everybody already knows something about relativity only they don't know how much they already know until they see a picture like this.

It will be interesting to hear what the McVicker's management has to say about how the Einstein picture goes over or goes under with its customers.

June 15, 1923

Safety Last

Harold Lloyd's latest release, Safety Last, has opened with an eye on summer prospects at Orchestra Hall. It is a six-reel picture presented with accompanying films from the most fascinating in the Pathé kitbag.

The large and growing number of Harold Lloyd fans will enjoy Safety Last. It is full of the tricks which have

---

*Only 38 with Lois Wilson, directed by William De Mille, C.B.'s brother.

earned him his friends, and in some scenes he is probably
funnier than in any previous picture.

He is seen working in a department store as a clerk.
Bargain counter rushers are tearing his coat and necktie off,
so the floorwalker reports him and he is warned to make a
more presentable appearance.   About this time a girl enters--
from his hometown--the girl he is engaged to marry.   He
has written her about the important position he holds and how
much money he is putting by so they can soon marry.   She
congratulates him on his rapid advancement.   He carries on
a bluff that he is a floorwalker and still later that he is the
general manager of the store.   He sends her to her hotel in
a wealthy customer's limousine.

A bad end he would have come to only he made an ar-
rangement with the general manager of the store to bring
hundreds of people to the store, prospective customers.   He
was trying his hand at what the general manager called "ex-
ploitation."   But it happened that the "human fly" he contracted
with to climb the outside of the store walls couldn't come so
he had to be this "human fly" himself.

Mildred Davis*, Bill Strothers and Walcott D. Clark
are in the supporting cast.   The picture was directed by
Fred Newmeyer** and Sam Taylor.

June 1, 1923

Critic's Choice

A communication from a woman movie-goer takes ex-
ception to our handling of Nazimova's Salome, and before
coming to that particular point, registers this opinion:

"It seems to me that I have never read worse criticisms
of the movies than yours--so mechanical, wooden and wrong-
headed.   How anyone could praise the things you do, and then

---

*Davis (1901-1969) would soon retire from films after mar-
rying Harold Lloyd.

**Newmeyer (1888-?) was a professional baseball player
before becoming a screen writer and director.

come down on a production like Nazimova's Salome--a play
so exquisitely artistic and original, is more than I can see.
There must be a screw loose about you."

This communication was signed by Jane Morris, giving
no street address. At the same time, another communica-
tion arrived from another woman movie-goer, registering
this opinion:

"Your motion picture criticisms, as you are probably
aware yourself, do not tell the truth about the art in the
photoplays. The art is silly and degrading. You could per-
form a service such as Bernard Shaw did for the stage in
London, if you would be frank."

Taking up the first communication first, we notice that
the writer objects to reviews on the ground that they are
mechanical, wooden, wrong-headed. It may be that the prop-
er rejoinder is, "Are movies, which move mechanically,
woodenly, wrong-headedly, worth reviews which are vital,
golden, right-minded?" If a film is stupid, does it deserve
brilliant writing? Or, rather, if a film is dull and wooden,
should the reviewer say to himself, "This is where I get a
warmth all over; now is the time for all men to come to the
aid of their party; this is where we start educating the ex-
hibitors, the producers, the directors, the scenario writers,
the taste of the public, the integrity of the nation, the habits
of our ancestors."

The reviewer has his choice; he can say that to him-
self, or he can do his best at cheerfully telling whether he
thinks the film is decidedly one worth going to see, or wheth-
er it is just so-so, and it makes no difference whether any-
body goes or whether it is plain rotten, and not worth a look.

As for doing for the movies in Chicago what Bernard
Shaw did for the stage in London, the answer is there is only
one London, only one Bernard Shaw, and what he has done
for London in his lifetime may be measured by the changes
in stage art which have come since the time he began writ-
ing and the time of the present hour.

Maybe we might add this one fact for to-day: Criticism
of motion pictures having simultaneous national circulation is
different from criticism of local stage plays, different from
forty angles.

June 16, 1923

Movies' Metamorphosis

Along with occasional reading of the New York review-
ers of the movies--such as Heywood Broun and John Farrar*
--we take a look regularly at Capper's Weekly, the Kansas
farm paper which is read from end to end of the Corn Belt.

And we noticed this week the opinion hot off the bat in
that paper: "The movies are getting decidedly better."

The easy sneer at the movies is passing away. The
refined snort of cavalier contempt for the film drama is not
quite like it used to be. A change has come.

This has different causes, reasons, explanations and
facts behind the happening of it.

First of all, the picture industry has been centered in
a few large organizations. They saw a tremendous future
for the film if handled right. And they saw that a censorship
and a handling as stiff as that of the Volstead probibition law
would come along if the percentage of trash and hokum were
not cut down. That is part of the change.

Then, too, the producers, directors, players, photog-
raphers, scenario writers, have all been working in an
infant industry and art. They have learned more about tell-
ing stories on the screen; if a man is to take his coat off
he can be shown starting to take it off and the next showing
has him with it all the way off, the process of wriggling out
of the sleeves needn't be shown unless that action has some
feature of character. And so on.

The makers of the movies have been collaborating. They
have watched producers such as Charlie Chaplin, D.W. Griffith,
and later, James Cruze.

It is such current pictures as Down to the Sea in Ships,
The Covered Wagon, The Spoilers, Out of Luck, Salomy Jane,
Penrod and Sam that are responsible for the changing view-
point about the movies.

---

*Broun (1888-1939) was the famous columnist of the New
York World and Farrar (1892-1974) was the editor of The
Bookman.

When Heywood Broun and John Farrar in New York
think so on the one hand and Capper's Weekly, the Kansas
farm paper, which is read from end to end of the Corn Belt,
says so, on the other hand, it is a sign of change.

Aug. 4, 1923

Chaplin vs. Lloyd George

Charlie Chaplin is set to arrive in the city to-day, while
it happens also that David Lloyd George is set to arrive.

These are two very interesting men to take notice of
the modern civilization in which we live.

Of course, there are people who will say at once that
Lloyd George is a high, important, consequential figure who
should hardly be mentioned along with Charlie Chaplin.

And at the same time there are many other people who
have a suspicion that they have heard sometime of this man,
Lloyd George, connected with some government in Europe,
while these same people have a feeling that they know all
about Charlie Chaplin, a feeling as though he lived next door
to them and they have seen his shirts on the wash line.

Two very interesting men, Lloyd George and Charlie
Chaplin. Both of them speak to millions of people. The
sun is always rising or setting somewhere over the earth,
on their wide-flung audience.

Many differences could be found between these two men
who speak to millions. From the motion picture standpoint
it is interesting to notice that Chaplin has two advantages
over Lloyd George.

Chaplin has millions of people looking at his pictures,
who are never reached by the speeches of Lloyd George.

There are millions of people over the earth who can-
not read. The only way they could understand one of Lloyd
George's speeches would be for someone else to read it to
them while they listened. But these same millions of people
can sit and look at a Chaplin picture--and understand Chaplin's
message--whatever that message may be.

The motion picture language in the way Chaplin uses it
is a wonderful and simple speech. It reaches millions who
don't know the ABC or the XYZ of their languages. They
can't spell c-a-t nor r-a-t. But they talk about Charlie
Chaplin as they do about Santa Claus or the Devil or the god
who makes rain.

Then there are the millions of people over the earth who
never read the English language because they have never learned
that language. They were born and they grew up learning to
speak Spanish, French, German, Russian, Chinese, Japanese,
Kamchatkan, Abyssinian and so on. The only way they could
understand a speech by Lloyd George would be for somebody
else to translate it and read the translation and they would
be suspicious of the translator.

But the motion picture, however, doesn't need any trans-
lation. It can be understood by everybody except those who
are blind or have something wrong with their eyes so that
they can't see the picture as it flickers past on the screen.
There are millions of these people who don't read the English
language who sit and look at the Chaplin film and read Charlie
Chaplin's message--whatever that message may be.

Of course, the main point where the argument comes
in is on the point of whether Chaplin has messages and wis-
dom as important to deliver as Lloyd George. On that point
there can be argument. There are friends of Chaplin who
believe their argument for his case is stronger than that of
the friends of Lloyd George.

The difference between these two men who speak to
millions was pointed out in another connection, one time by
Abraham Lincoln.

The difference between them is the same as that be-
tween a horse chestnut and a chestnut horse. Both are men,
but one is an artist and the other a statesman.

Oct. 16, 1923

The Hunchback of Notre Dame

In The Hunchback of Notre Dame may be seen what is

surely Lon Chaney's masterpiece, the best piece of character work he has done in his interesting life in the movies.

For one familiar with the famous novel by Victor Hugo, one of the warmest and grandest writers of the French language, there might be the feeling that it would be the strong, unshapely hunchback himself who would be the hardest part of the book to put on in a screen drama.

As it happens, however, the hunchback is the best figure of all the puppets, and the outstanding thing of the production.

It is a picture worth seeing; it is evident that Wallace Worsley*, the director, and others cared, and were painstaking, and lots of money was spent to make a big smash of a picture.

Yet the production falls far short of being a masterpiece somehow; with the exception of the hunchback, the characters and the masses of people and their action don't have the funny, crazy, rugged, massive, lovable human stuff that goes with the novel of Victor Hugo.

The beggars don't seem to have any secrets. So fine a character portraylist as Ernest Torrence**, doing the king of the beggars, only rarely gets into the proud, wild, isolated quality of a leader of tatterdemalions by natural right.

Patsy Ruth Miller*** as Esmeralda, the dancer and mascot of the beggars, does excellent work. There was capable direction of her and she added her own charm and intelligence. Tully Marshall**** does a good quizzical King Louis XI.

---

*Worsley (1880-1944) stopped directing shortly after sound pictures arrived.

**Torrence (1878-1933) was a Scot, and a one-time operatic star, who appeared in The Covered Wagon the same year.

***Miller (1905-1981) outgrew and more or less lived down such juvenile roles, becoming in time a minor leading lady.

****Marshall (1864-1943) appeared in a remarkable number of important films, from Intolerance in 1915 to The Unholy Garden in 1931 and This Gun For Hire shortly before his death.

But why should the subtitles be written by somebody who
does not know how to spell and who is ignorant of grammar?
Victor Hugo, for instance, had a contempt for grammatical
and correct speech, was an adept in slang. But Hugo did know
grammar. If he used the expression "from whence" he did
it on purpose, knowing he was ungrammatical, which is not
the case in the subtitles of this picture.

And why spell forsworn wrong? Why not use some
other word you know how to spell rather than bluff?

And among thieves and murderers they don't say "I'll
slit your throat," they say, "I'll slit your windpipe." They
use the word windpipe instead of throat on such an occasion.

There were other slips indicating pretenses to culture
that are full of holes and apertures similar to well-known
cheeses.

The director, the scenario writer of this picture, didn't
love his people and understand them in quite the way that
Victor Hugo did.

Lon Chaney's rise to stardom has been a struggle against
handicaps, the kind of a story that has grit and stamina in
every line of it. Chaney contends that there is nothing ex-
traordinary in his life, that it's simply been a hard life. He
will talk of men's things, of prize fights, races, business-
men's and fellow artists' success, but of Lon Chaney's early
struggles he says little. Therefore, it was no small achieve-
ment to get him to give the following facts:

"I've fought-fought-fought for everything that is mine,"
Chaney once told an interviewer. "I starved, I labored and
I hungered for the glad hand, for the companionship that
speeds so many young fellows on their way to success. I've
often wondered why I kept on, why I shouldn't have given up
and drifted, as I saw many others doing. But there was
something in me that wouldn't let me stop."

Not handsome, of a somewhat somber nature, his face
is stern even in repose, and his words carry conviction be-
cause of the utter lack of affectation. He continued his story.

"My parents were deaf-mutes, but perfectly normal in

every other way and possessed of good minds. So, as a
child, I learned to express every wish with my facial muscles.
I could talk with my fingers before I could speak, but as I
grew older, I found that it was unnecessary as we could con-
verse with our faces, with our eyes. Those early years of
pantomime are responsible for whatever skill I have at pres-
ent.

"When I was 18 I landed a job as stagehand in a Colorado
Springs theater. Later I was a combination stagehand, chorus
man and wardrobe mistress, yes, mistress, all for the stu-
pendous sum of $14 a week. I was supporting my parents
and brother and sister.

"I played in comic opera when I wanted to do tragic
opera. I danced for the money, not for the joy. I danced
in The Time, the Place, and the Girl, The Royal Chef, and
other operas. Nine years ago I went into pictures. My first
part was the heavy in Hell Morgan's Girl. I had no one to
teach me to make up. I had to teach myself by observing
characters on the street and seeking to copy them.

"After five years with Universal I decided to free-lance.
I was determined to play only roles that I believed offered me
real opportunity. My big chance came in The Miracle Man.
Then I went back to Universal to do the part of Lissard in
The Penalty.

"However, now I am through with cripple roles. Though
I have played men of every nationality, I prefer Orientals.
The Latin races are too expressive, they talk with their hands,
with gestures, but portraying the Oriental is to my mind an
art."

The most prized possession of this man of a thousand
faces is the makeup box. It is better described as a small-
size steamer trunk--and contains the most amazing collection
of appliances for character makeup. False eyebrows and
beards of all descriptions, false teeth which slip on over his
own, tiny glass tubes to distend his nostrils, and tape, used
to draw his face into all kinds of queer grimaces.

Chaney's portrayal of Quasimodo, the "Hunchback of
Notre Dame" in Hugo's masterpiece at the Harris, has elicited
unbounded praises.

Nov. 9, 1923

Jackie Coogan

Jackie Coogan is forever and ever "The Kid." The
imprint of Charlie Chaplin upon the hands, the feet, the face,
the mind of this little boy is evidently to last as long as
Jackie lasts. This influence of Chaplin, overlaying a certain
rare intelligence and brain genius all his own, make Master
Coogan a rare thing in any world. It is gossiped in film
circles that David Belasco drooping his long white chin upon
his dominie's collar thoughtfully said, "This young Coogan
boy: he will someday be America's greatest actor. When
he is a man he will be the leader of his profession."

He is unspoiled because he has never known anything
else but adulation and praise. Practically born backstage, he
is of the theater world completely, entirely. Acting is what
he knows, what he thinks, what he hears. It is work, it is
play, it is life. And it shows plainly every foot of the way
in Long Live the King, which his parents have adapted from
Mary Roberts Rinehart's novel for a $600,000 production,
playing now at the Chicago Theater.

There are no standards of criticism for a Coogan picture.
The human instinct of love and preservation for its young
makes Jackie outside all ordinary standards. You love him,
you feel queer stabs at the heart, strange tremors of affection,
unreasoning partisanship for his gallant, seriocomic adventures
whether he is in rags or robes. Yet Jackie is winning his
way up on his talents and not his personality. Out of the haze
of affection with which the American public regards him
is rising a definite pillar of admiration for his art. He is a
great kid but a greater little actor in Long Live the King, a
tale of a runaway prince of Bulgaria, plots to kill him, dyna-
miters, intrigues of court, and love tangles behind the throne.
The plot often wanders off and leaves him, the other actors
fail him, but who knows or cares. Jackie is himself. Rosemary
Theby, Alan Hale, Alan Forrest and others are faithfully the
characters the director asked for. Jackie will be himself
plus the undying influence of Chaplin until he dies.

Dec. 13, 1923

Child Stars and Salaries

The little children are leading items in the movies now-

adays. Salaries for juvenile actors are rising while salaries
for adult actors are going down in Hollywood. Producers
are economizing wherever they can, but they can't save on
children's salaries. It doesn't pay. People want boy stars
and more of them. Girls? Yes, but not so many. Little
girls as a rule are too self-conscious to act well.

Baby Peggy is the exception. She has the Jackie Coogan
talent for self-forgetfulness in a part, the same big-eyed ab-
sorption in whatever is at hand.

When pictures were in their infancy they used no in-
fants. Now when they are in their adolescence they need
infants badly, and indeed will pay high to try out babies who
are born with just the right expression on their faces and
just the right curves to their bodies.

Only Chaplin, Fairbanks, Pickford, Meighan* and Norma
Talmadge exceed 8-year-old Jackie Coogan in salary. Young
Ben Alexander**, who is now 11, ranks up with Owen and
Matt Moore, Colleen Moore*** and Milton Sills in weekly sal-
ary. Buddy Messenger is close behind. Little George Marion
has leaped into high figures lately. The salary drawn by
Frecides Barry before he outgrew his little boyhood was enor-
mous. "Peaches" Jackson, Frankie Lee, Newton Hall need
never worry about their future. The money is banked already.

But the new sensation is the salaries and the scores of
youngsters who race and tear through the "kid" comedies
which crowd the screens today. Fat boys, freckled boys,
"sissy" boys, all kinds of boys are needed and scouts go
through the country hunting them. Special arrangements for
their education, for their shelter from the spirit that some-
times grips adult actors, nurses, tutors, duennas surround
them. That pays, the filmmakers have found out.

Ben Alexander, for instance, can only be free for studio

---

*That is, Thomas Meighan (1879-1936).

**Alexander (1911-1969) survived childhood and sound pic-
tures to become Jack Webb's on-screen partner in the tele-
vision series Dragnet.

***Owen Moore (1887-1939) was once married to Mary
Pickford; three of his brothers, including Matt (1888-1960),
were also actors; Colleen Moore (b. 1900) is no relation.

work at certain times. His lessons come first. Parents
see to that and the directors cooperate. They say that it
took two weeks longer to film Booth Tarkington's story, Boy
of Mine, because Ben Alexander's lessons kept him out of
the studio certain hours of the morning and made the other
actors idle. But the makers say it was worth it to keep the
boy natural and fresh.

What these little individuals will be when they grow up
is of course a question. Many theatrical men and dramatists
look for them to develop a screen technique that is beyond
anything conceived now, an adaptability to the peculiar flicker
and flow of screen rhythm that is unseen by actors who went
into the new movies from the stage. Thirty years from to-
day will tell the story.

                                                Dec. 15, 1923

                          Will Rogers

The case of Will Rogers and the movies is a case by
which one might prove a good deal about American art and
American culture of the present time.

The big main reason Rogers left the movies was be-
cause he was too homely and horsey and plain and unvarnished.

He can ride the toughest broncos in the gang, he is a
past master of the lasso, horses love him and go wild about
him, but the most of the women going to the movies don't.

He has rich humor; he is a salty American wit, and
friends of his have said, "Will, you would be all right in the
pictures--only you know too much--you're too smart."

Well, all of this sort of leads up to Will Rogers' latest
release in the movies. It is a little 10-minute affair titled
Uncensored Movies.

Mainly it consists of parodies or burlesques on some
of the famous stars. The one of Tom Mix is a masterpiece
of humor. We can see Tom Mix himself laughing at it.

He rides the horse, Tony, and the pursuers in motorcars with speedometers registering ninety miles an hour can't catch the man on horseback.

A jackrabbit running alongside is losing breath, so the horseman leans down and picks up the rabbit and gives it a rest.

Coming to a crossroad he changes a sign so it reads wrong and four pursuing motorcars eventually one by one topple over the edge of a precipice and turn somersaults before they hit bottom.

Then back he goes to where his sweetheart has been kidnapped; he jumps his horse across several wide chasms and arrives at the cabin where the kidnapper has the girl. A whole gang engages him there in a hand-to-hand encounter. He conquers them all with his swift and adroit boxing and wrestling.

One of the hot buns amidst the movies--a sort of cream puff of human intelligence--is this Uncensored Movies by Will Rogers.

We hope Rogers will live long and have health, doing what he pleases to do, because he is one of our worthwhile national possessions.

Dec. 31, 1923

Technological advances proved to be powerful catalysts for Hollywood. Not only was the talkie just around the corner, but panchromatic film came into general use, beginning the era of personal cinematographic styles. Gone were the days in which reliance on exterior shooting, a shallow depth of focus, and heavy makeup were unavoidable.

All the news was not good for filmmakers: by 1924 radio established itself as a mass, free entertainment. As would be the case with television in the 1950's, the movie box office was affected and Hollywood fought back. One weapon was a continued tone of European "culture" through imported artists. Another was the lavish epic which radio could not match. The best example--and one which Sandburg liked very much--was Douglas Fairbanks' The Thief of Bagdad which took seven months to shoot and fourteen months to complete, employing 4,000 extras and six-and-one-half acres of sets.

Sandburg, for his part, was continuing work on his own epic, a Lincoln biography which eventually would encompass a million and a half words over six volumes and would win a Pulitzer Prize.

Victor Seastrom

In movie circles around town they are chuckling about the way Victor Seastrom, a Swedish director, came to Hollywood and spoiled a pet idea out there.

A pet idea of a lot of American directors was to have

fancy, pretty and illogical lights shining on the actors from
places where lights in life never are. Many directors throw
bright cross lights on a man sitting under a lamp reading a
book or on a girl in her dressing room with only one window
in it. They have thought it didn't matter where the lights
came from if the picture was pretty.

Seastrom, who has done strong, realistic pictures in
Sweden, came to Hollywood to do Name the Man for Goldwyn.
He came in silent, kindly, and did things his own way. Amer-
ican directors gave him advice as he became one of the tetrarchs
of the camera and showed him how to light his sets.

Seastrom smiled and went on doing things his own way.
He had an idea. This was that everything in a picture must
be reasonable, that if a girl sat in a room where there was
only one window all the light would naturally come through
that window. There were to be no tricks with the camera
and kliegs just to make things pretty.

He made his picture that way. He talked to the actors
that way. Film men who have seen the picture say the ac-
tors must have got his idea; that they show in their acting
that there is a reason for what they do; that their hands and
feet and eyes show you what their heads are thinking.

Seastrom, the whisper is, gets a queer feeling into
his people with his heavy, kindly voice, talking, talking,
talking--something the way Griffith works.

Seastrom doesn't like megaphones or caps turned back-
ward or leather puttees. He was an actor once, rated as
Sweden's best, and his voice leads his actors now into slow,
certain moods. He made Mae Busch cry real tears in the
murder trial scene where she hears her fate booming down
from the bench, they say.

These are things one hears from movie men who saw
him work. Whatever there is of this in the picture will be
seen when it unreels at the Chicago Theater next week. At
any rate Seastrom has made a stir in Hollywood where it
takes something nowadays to make a stir.

Feb. 2, 1924

Where D.W. Griffith uses the feet of girls--nervous,

shy, gesticulating story-telling feet--to put across his picture points, Victor Seastrom, who has come to America with the title "The Griffith of Europe," uses hands.

Hands express his thoughts and feelings. He focuses his camera on fingers that clutch, relax, flutter and grip.

When an old man dies all one sees is the hands suddenly go limp. Life seeps out of his fingertips and is gone.

Bessie Collister, the working girl heroine, is introduced by a close-up of her hands, drawing on cheap gloves, excited, lowly hands. When she succumbs to temptation one sees her hand stealing around the neck of a man--no close-ups, nothing more.

Seastrom is a great maker of pictures, understanding his medium with surety and genius. Quiet, telling symbolism and a magnificent gift for making his people human and full of character, give Seastrom's first American picture, Name the Man, high rating and significance among pictures to-day.

His characters move logically and forcefully and the people who play them--Conrad Nagel, Mae Busch, DeWitt Jennings, Patsy Ruth Miller and others of Hollywood--will seem to you strangely unlike themselves. Their familiar identities are gone. Under Seastrom's direction their mannerisms, looks, habits of acting vanish. They are new to themselves so completely they are, for the time, the people of Seastrom's imagination.

The story is an adaptation of Sir Hall Caine's Master of Man, and is from the Goldwyn studios.

We should prophesy on the strength of Seastrom's start, as high a place for him in America as he earned in Sweden.

Feb. 6, 1924

The Birth of a Nation in Retrospect

The Birth of a Nation has a peculiar standing among motion-picture plays. There is probably no other photoplay that rates so highly as an artistic production which at the same time has so low a rating as history.

If a boy or girl or a young man or woman should ask this reviewer if The Birth of a Nation is good, reliable American history, this reviewer would answer that it is about the same kind of good, reliable American history as Uncle Tom's Cabin.

Just as the author of Uncle Tom's Cabin was a sensitive Connecticut woman*, who saw slavery as a terrible wrong and presented her viewpoint in a terribly exciting book, so the author of The Birth of a Nation is a sensitive Kentuckian who saw the Reconstruction period after the war as full of terrible wrongs and he has presented his viewpoint in a terribly exciting photoplay.

David Wark Griffith puts on the screen the wrongs of the South as he heard them from the lips of his home people as a boy--just as Harriet Beecher Stowe put into Uncle Tom's Cabin the wrongs of Christian America as she heard them from the lips of brothers and kinsmen as she built a home and gave birth to seven children and felt a sacredness attaching to all human flesh.

Thus far, we have seen no screen version of Uncle Tom's Cabin. But we can almost imagine that if a child or young man or woman should be shown a good photoplay of Uncle Tom's Cabin after seeing The Birth of a Nation it might be the case that the student would say, "The history of the United States seems kind of mixed when we get it this way."

And we may as well admit that putting the history of the United States on the motion pictures is a hard and mixed job.

We wish all luck to Griffith in the film, America, which he is now working on. We hope it will be more strictly accurate, that it will be the hummer of a melodrama which is to be seen in The Birth of a Nation.

Feb. 20, 1924

---

*Harriet Beecher Stowe (1811-1896) was born in Litchfield, Connecticut.

A Son of the Sahara

The sheiks are recurrent. Picture makers seem to
feel that people want some more of the Valentino brand of
Arab lovers.

So Edwin Carewe took American players to Algiers,
where the camels are so much a bunch and the riders cheaper
than in Hollywood and the Sahara real. Atmosphere was what
he gained by going there. Some shots against the sun across
the desert are worth going to Africa to get.

A Son of the Sahara Carewe calls it. It is what you
would expect, a rip-roaring Arab chieftain, equally at home
in evening clothes or a midnight tent, kidnapping a cutie and
holding her a captive but not a slave.

You would expect harem scenes, plural and multiple and
additional wives lolling around the seraglio, playing with gui-
tars and goldfish and spatting with each other. They are in
A Son of the Sahara.

You would expect the sheik to be scorned by the lovely
white lady because he is black. Arabs are always accused
of being black in pictures and fiction, although racially they
are white if you want to be scientific. And you would expect
the sheik to go through with his fiery plans until the patrician
lady weeps and says she loves him and this makes a gentle-
man out of him. And you would be confident he wouldn't be
black after all, but a kidnapped child of European parents
reared among the wild tribes.

Just what you expect happens. So A Son of the Sahara
will satisfy those who want a good tingly sheik picture again.
Carewe satisfies those but he never surprised anybody. Melo-
drama he can do, character building he cannot.

Production is by First National and the showing is at
the Chicago Theater where quite a stage production is seen
with it. Whoever did the color lighting on the prologue must
have been born when an April rainbow was in the sky. He
is an artist and as some people say "notin' else but."

April 22, 1924

Cecil B. De Mille

The news today is that Cecil B. De Mille has learned about medieval history.

He used to know only ancient myths and legends and cavemen, and jungle gents occupied his "cutbacks" into the past whenever he put on something a little fancy to illustrate why modern gents act the way they do.

Cecil B. De Mille only cuts back as far as Romeo and Juliet now and then for a flash to show the 1924 brand of hero singing up at a balcony in Shakespeare's clothes.

This little diversion is unimportant to the picture and is mentioned only to show a pleasant widening of Mr. De Mille's range.

Triumph is this film--Ziegfeld's new picture--and it has settings and decorations as splendid and story as unconvincing as any of his other modern comedy dramas. Triumph is about two half-brothers and a handsome young Juno who is a forewoman in their canning factory. The better half of the brothers starts as a loafer and ends up president of the canning factory; the worser half of the brothers starts as president and ends up as just a plain canner. The young woman loses her ambition to be a great singer when a fire ruins her voice and would have wound up as just a plain canner too if the better half of the brothers hadn't married her.

Granting that the story isn't like life, it can be claimed for it that it is technically perfect, that it makes audiences laugh, and that it is excellently acted. Rod LaRocque* is, as in The Ten Commandments, a fine young player going to his work with a lean, picturesque vigor that makes him a rival of Valentino. Leatrice Joy justifies the stardom that is soon to be hers and Victor Varconi, a newcomer from Europe, gives a striking performance. Other names you will know are Charles Ogle, Theodore Kosloff**, Robert Edeson, Julia Faye, George Fawcett, Raymond Hatton, Alma Bennett and ZaSu Pitts.

---

*Rod LaRocque was the professional name of one Roderick la Rocque de la Rour (1896-1969), a one-time circus star.

**Kosloff (1882-1956) had been a member of the Russian Imperial Ballet before coming to the U.S. in 1912.

Production is by Paramount at McVickers.

April 30, 1924

De Mille's Golden Bed

The Golden Bed is a good title for the picture it tops.
The name keys everything for you, suggesting just what you
would expect Cecil B. De Mille to have in mind when he sat
him down to figure: "Now, just what does the public want?
Ease, luxury, gorgeousness, society, a little love, a little
kiss."

Down South the slaves used to moon and dream about
golden slippers, their feet wore out tramping up and down
cotton rows in a blistering sun, so they gave up joy as a
prospective pleasure of this world and took their satisfaction
out of imagining a future life where their feet would be cool
and easy and fine in slippers of gold.

De Mille's Golden Bed is what he imagines a toiling
world to be fondest of--a vast and gorgeous couch where one
may lie all day with no alarm clocks or dying furnaces or
yowling children to be calling him or her away. The name
suggests the dream of Kingdom Come which Mr. De Mille would
dope out for the workers in the greatest nation of workers
since time began.

No matter if the girl who slept on the golden bed was
punished for her selfishness and idleness; no matter if the
long sweet, beauty sleep she took there got her nothing at
the finale, De Mille's work is done, his idea is "over" when
he shows the lovely Lillian Rich snoozing in the cool eiderdown
of the golden bed. The emphasis has been made; the showman
has hit his mark.

Right in line with this ornate idea--and De Mille, better
than any other director, knows how to decorate with photog-
raphy and art-lighting, such an idea--is a lid-tilting, Goliath
of a ball. De Mille grinds slowly, but he grinds exceedingly
fine on these ballroom stunts. He has had girls bathing in
champagne, racing on the backs of their escorts and all that
revel sort of thing. But in his new picture which reels
across McVicker's screen, he now has a "candy" ball, a gi-

gantic society party where the furnishings, the decorations,
the furniture, the walls, the pillars, the sofa cushions are
of candy, and the actors, it is felt, might well be of the
same material. An extravagant, preposterous idea, which
is evidently what Mr. De Mille thinks the dreams of children
are.

Add to this a touch of melodrama wherein people climb
glaciers of ice to find little love flowers in the crevices, and
fall in the process, string these gaudy incidents on a thin mor-
ality story and you have The Golden Bed--typically De Mille,
weak where De Mille is always weak, effective where De Mille
is always effective--in his photography.

Rod La Rocque, Robert Cain, Warner Baxter and Henry
B. Walthall* are the men--good actors all. Lillian Rich and
Vera Reynolds have the main girl roles and handle them ar-
tificially but gracefully.

Dec. 20, 1924

Tom Mix on Skis

Tom Mix comes again--and now in a picture called The
Trouble Shooter.

If recollection serves us correctly, this is the first time
we have seen Mr. Mix on skis.

Also we have not before noticed him--if recollection
serves us correctly--up on a telegraph pole fixing the wire
while a storm rages about him.

---

*The career of Walthall (1878-1936) is one of the era's
most intriguing. He was the son of a Confederate captain
and plantation owner and is himself best known for his role
as the Little Colonel in The Birth of a Nation when he was
part of Griffith's permanent company. But his career dete-
riorated to the point where he left Hollywood for vaudeville,
only to be given a fresh start in films after the introduction
of talkies--the reverse of what happened to so many of his
contemporaries.

Few dangers and few outdoor sports remain in which Tom Mix can't be seen in a film without repeating on his past.

Yet it is doubted whether any Mix fan or folks who enjoy Western danger and hardship pictures will not again enjoy the Mixian mixes here seen.

The Mix mixes seen before are here--the peril to be braved, the race to be run, the girl to be won--and the horse, Tony, and his rider beating big odds and coming through winners.

The going is good.

We don't know just how Tom Mix keeps on producing so many photoplays with a clean breath to them with stories not tiresome, though all somewhat alike, and with a balance of danger and fun.

But he does it.

Kathlyn Key is a new woman to play opposite him. Opinion will be different about her. We like her. She doesn't overplay.

The all and many who have hitherto enjoyed Mix, must again see him in The Trouble Shooter. Its first run is at the Monroe Theater this week.

May 9, 1924

Westerns

The western pictures keep going. The riding and shooting hero, with a background of Rocky Mountains or the Sierras-- is always wanted.

Styles come and go in vampires and working-girls, in sheiks and Romeos, in villians who look the part and devils who don't.

But "Ride 'em Cowboy" always goes.

It is as American as the American flag.

And there is one noticeable thing among these westerns. That is, some of the actors are terrific and steady workers.

Take Tom Mix, Buck Jones and Hoot Gibson--three riders who do their own riding and never need a double for a rodeo.

They are among the most tireless workers in our country.

It seems as though they are no sooner done with one picture than they have begun the next.

They take their vacations making pictures.

If they let up on riding before the camera, and climbing hand over hand up a rope till they reach the top of the mountain butte, they simply lose appetite, suffer from loss of sleep and cry for the camera, calling through the megaphone, "We're ready now--get into that."

Their work is not what a critic would class in the output of first-rate genius. But they are producing first-rate entertainment--and always clean--and what with their audience of millions--and especially the young and impressionable --they have an importance as artists, these smiling and wholesome young bucks, Tom Mix, Buck Jones and Hoot Gibson.

For they are bucks--bucks that ride bucking horses and sawbucks--and they are young and will all three die young, no matter how long they live. It's the riding, the horses, the mountains that does it--and the kids that enjoy their pictures.

June 21, 1924

Early Sound

The phonofilm, the Lee DeForest* invention showing at McVicker's Theater, is one of those American jokes with an edge to it.

---

*DeForest (1873-1961) had invented a radio wave amplifier in 1906; his photofilm experiments of 1919-1924 were the first successful attempts at some form of synchronized sound on motion picture film.

It has the look of the joke of the first horseless carriage, the first wireless communication experiments.

Wheezes and mistakes go along with the operation of it.

It is amusing in the way that a child learning to walk is amusing.

The human voice is not delivered with clear tones--but the synchronism is surprising.

The lips of the speaker are certainly shaping the words which we occasionally catch, and against prejudice we come to the feeling that the screen is talking, sending sounds to our ears just as it is sending pictures to our eyes.

They are shrews in their arrangement of the details of the demonstration.

We are shown a dancer dancing without music; the senorita looks like a movie Spaniard; then there is a shift from the silversheet to the phonofilm and the senorita is dancing to good music, not missing a bar of the pizzicato.

A banjo orchestra goes through the motions of playing; they look silly; then from silversheet we pass to phonofilm and they are gay.

The steady drive is on to make talking movies.

That will be slow in coming; it would mean adding all the difficulties of real art to the art of pantomime.

But--music and dancing will come first.

The saxophone player now showing in this initial phonofilm has an added charm, his playing has an extra vitality for us, because we see him blowing his breath, and executing facial and bodily rhythms going with his music.

July 19, 1924

Stereoscopiks

If you happened to see "Stereoscopiks" offered at any

theater you may be passing the next few weeks, you will find one or two reels of strange fun mixed with science.

It is a showing of binocular or two-eye photography in place of the common single-eye photography of the motion picture.

The camera blinks with two lenses, about as far apart as the two human eyes, and the audience looks at the picture with spectacles furnished by the ushers.

The extra keen vision of two eyes is brought out in a startling way.

Objects and people move out from the screen straight toward the onlooker so that there is almost an illusion that we could reach out and take hold of what is projected toward us.

This apparatus and what it does is just now a sort of toy or novelty. We laugh at the newness and peculiarity of it, just as fifteen years back we laughed at a motion picture of people walking and running.

But when we consider what toil and experiment there is going on to improve this apparatus, we have the feeling that in five, ten, or twenty years, we may all carry pocket stereoscopes, or receive the glasses at the door, for looking at motion picture plays presented in three dimensions, with the same projection of surfaces in depth, that we have in everyday life.

If to such an apparatus there should then be added the reproduction of sound, the projection of voices in a way perfected and improved over the points now attained, that would be the triple novelty of motion and speech presented in three dimensions.

We would advise all 100 per cent movie fans to try and hang on to life ten or twenty years more.

We'll see what we'll see.

Sept. 6, 1924

Adolphe Menjou and the Censors

The film playing of Adolphe Menjou is probably the thing most talked of among the topics of moviegoers these current days.

Since the time Menjou had a prominent role in Charlie Chaplin's first, last and only eight-reel picture, Menjou has stood forth as a rare article in the language of pantomime.

He says some things plainly, and insinuates and implies other things vaguely and indefinitely with a shrug of the left shoulder or a trick of the right eyebrow.

He does the main heavy work of the picture, Sinners in Silk, having its first run at the Chicago Theater this week.

Eleanor Boardman, Conrad Nagel and Miss Du Pont are in the supporting cast, with Miss Boardman proving an excellent vis-à-vis for Menjou.

The moviemakers know they are tackling a difficult theme when they try to show a man of the world inviting a young unmarried woman to a dinner in his little garden home on top of a New York skyscraper, where just they two alone are to have soup, roast, lettuce and wine, at windows looking down on the blinking electric signs of Broadway.

They work it out pretty well, as the story skates on its thin ice, which was measured with a watchful eye by the censors.

The climax comes with a bang that is not loud nor noisy, but is nevertheless a bang.

The picture is a Metro-Goldwyn, directed by Hobart Henley.

Aug. 29, 1924

The Thief of Bagdad

Impossible, extravagant, full of thieves, liars, fine

clothes, fighters, monsters, a magic carpet, a crystal ball,
a golden apple, and a magic chest, beyond belief and yet per-
suasive, this is The Thief of Bagdad.

Not only is it the best production which has come from
Douglas Fairbanks in his extended motion picture career--it
is also one of the few sure film classics, one of the rare
and surprising creations of the film world.

Very seldom in motion pictures does one hesitate for
lavish phrases to properly hit off a picture.

But this is one of that kind, clean, brave, breathtaking,
impossible.

The youngest of children who can understand a plainly
told nonsense story, also the eldest graybeard who has been
thrust about by the cunning double-dealing of life's phantasma-
goria, both must find in The Thief of Bagdad much charm and
glory.

"Happiness must be earned," it tells us to begin and
end with.   Tunnels of tigers, a man-eating ape, a fire-breath-
ing dragon, a clammy-clawed sea monster, these are here.

Also the valley of fire and the white pavilions in the
moors.

Also Doug riding a slow galloping white horse over the
tops of clouds.

Two and seventy Arabian and Persian tales, aged 3,000
years, are compressed in this two hour and a half film perfor-
mance.

Outside of Charlie Chaplin's performance this looks to
us like the healthiest, boldest, most original and inspired
work that has come from the film-making world since the art
and industry of the cinema began doing business.

Seldom do we say, "Go--go and see this picture."

But we say just that of The Thief of Bagdad.

Seldom do we say, "You are missing great art, grand
nonsense, and cunning little packages of the wisdom of life
if you don't see this picture."

But we say just that of The Thief of Bagdad.

Seldom does a picture have toil, dreams, skill, genius,
with story characterization, atmosphere, all in a fine, swift-
moving orchestration.

Yet such is The Thief of Bagdad.

This is one of the few masterpieces.

Among the players are Douglas Fairbanks, Snitz Edwards,
Julanne Johnson, Anna May Wong.

The initial showing at the Woods Theater last night was
a success forty ways.   And we hope the picture stays for a
long run.

Sept. 1, 1924

The Thief of Bagdad is now in the next to the last week
of its stay at the Woods Theater.

The picture has had an excellent run, is quitting be-
cause its theater lease has expired, and sometime is coming
back for another run.

The production is one of the few great achievements of
motion picture art and entertainment.   Perhaps only three or
four others ever made get into a class with it.

The scenario editor of the Douglas Fairbanks organiza-
tion, Lotta Woods, who wrote the continuity for The Thief of
Bagdad, has an interesting and thoughtful way of telling how
some of the work went on.   She writes to us:

"We submerged ourselves in all the known translations of
the Arabian Nights--Galland, Scott, Burton, Lane, Forster,
Hanley and Payne.   Our research director brought us author-
ities on architecture, ornamentation, furniture, rugs and in-
formation on many other points.   He got illustrations, de-
lightful old woodcuts and engravings.

"'Our hero,' said Mr. Fairbanks, 'must be Every Young
Man--of this age or of any age--who believes that happiness
is a quantity that can be stolen, who is selfish--at odds with

the world--rebellious toward conventions on which comfortable
human relations are based. '

"The photography started.   It was the opinion of Mr.
Fairbanks that the settings looked as if they were anchored
to the ground.

"They have not the right and airy quality we want, " he
said. "We must lift them off the earth."

"Then he asked for acres of polished pavement, capa-
ble of exquisite reflections.   Around this, the high walls,
the minarets and domes, the balconies and lodges and the long
stairways of our city of Bagdad were built.

"Then acres of concrete paving were laid, painted many
times with thick coats of black paint and then polished.   We
were forced to walk on this with rubber or felt-soled shoes.
No visitors no matter how distinguished escaped this rule, and
for all we know, duchesses and chimney sweeps may have
worn the same felt horrors.

"This nuisance in the shape of polished black gave us
in part that which we wanted.   Around it, or on four sides,
were the high silver walls of the city of Bagdad.   The re-
flections of these silver walls went deep into the polished
pavements.   So we had gleaming highlights above the base-
lines, which destroyed that appearance of solid foundation
which had been an eyesore to us.   To preserve and elaborate
upon this illusion, the painters were instructed to graduate
the silver walls from the lightest shade that could be called
silver to the darkest, mindful still of the same metal.   Thus
one saw a city not quite of earth--a city with silver gleaming
at its feet.

"Our photographer had reflectors as high as the side of
a house, diffusers of various sizes and density, and studied
the position of the sun in relation to the location to be shot
at various times of the day.

"He had in view the tints and tones he would use on the
finished print; uranium, sepia, rose and that uncanny green
that we say presages something cataclysmic in the weather
line. "

Oct. 21, 1924

Wild Youth

Of all the film productions presenting the so-called
wild youth of what is known as the age of jazz, we suppose
the prize for this month can go to Wine of Youth showing at
the Chicago Theater this week.

Young, zippy, upper class people are shown eager and
bursting for life and more life and how to go to it.

To begin with, we have the girl of 1870 who danced the
polka till she was dizzy. Then comes her daughter of 1897,
dizzy with the waltz. After which we meet the dizzy whirlers
of the age of jazz, which is now.

A young man with a system is shown. If a girl won't
kiss him he puts on high speed, drives the car sixty miles
an hour, heads the car for a big tree, makes a quick nifty
stop, and the breathless girl kisses him her thanks.

A girl who takes aboard more liquor than she can carry
slides down a banister and steps around on a dance floor,
holding an umbrella over her.

The high spot comes when Mary tells her folks she
and a young man, and another couple, are going to a camp
and live with each other, unchaperoned, so as to find out if
they can, whether they are suited to each other and fit for
marriage.

Mary creeps back in the early dawn of the morning
after, rueful and repentant, to find her old-fashioned parents
in a hot squabble, indicating that the old folks are not author-
ities on the perfectly successful marriage.

Eleanor Boardman, Pauline Garron, William Collier,
Jr., William Haines, Bob Lyons and Robert Agnew are the
leading players. It is a First National picture, directed by
King Vidor Jr.

The scenario is from a stage play by Rachel Crothers.

Sept. 11, 1924

The Covered Wagon

While The Covered Wagon is being exhibited at a num-
ber of the large neighborhood theaters, it may be that cer-
tain moviegoers are asking themselves whether it is a pic-
ture worth seeing.

It is a question easy for a reviewer to answer, because
the picture is decidedly one of the worthy productions.

The story or idea which it tackles and holds for more
than two hours is one of the big ones of American history,
the nerve and audacity, the pluck and the vision of the men,
women and children who first crossed the great plains west
of the Mississippi, then the Rocky Mountains, the great des-
ert and the Sierra Mountains, for the purpose of settling the
Pacific coast country.

Of course the picture is intended as entertainment, and
as such could not tell all the hardships, could not show ac-
curately the atrocities of Indians on the white and the punish-
ment inflicted by the whites on the Indians.

Neither does the picture show a good deal of the life
in the covered wagons, when lack of laundry facilities, often
amid terrible dust storms, made cleanliness impossible for
cleanly people. There were "cooties" of the same sort as
in army life. And there were horse flies that bled the ani-
mals to blind rage.

Likewise there were trains of covered wagons that ran
out of food and left their skeletons of people and horses
along the trail.

These things, of course, in a picture intended first of
all to entertain, to make photoplay audiences forget their
troubles, would be impossible.

It is a case where actual history has to be softened
down and smoothed over, or else the makers of the picture
would never get back the $100,000 or so that they put into
it.

And yet the picture stands up among the most interest-
ing since the movies started winning their large daily audi-
ences.

The love story is told in a way that holds attention. The star players include Lois Wilson, Ernest Torrence, J. Warren Kerrigan, and the panorama of the long train of wagons winding over vast stretches of prairie and then amid mountain passes is a recurring theme that holds audiences in an extraordinary way.

Nov. 8, 1924

The Iron Horse

The Iron Horse, a Fox picture which opened its run at the Woods Theater Saturday night, is a story that dwells on the epic of the steam railroad and the locomotive crossing the great plains and connecting the Mississippi Valley with the Pacific Coast.

The opening scenes depict Abraham Lincoln about 1842 in Springfield, Illinois, bidding farewell to young people heading west. He makes predictions about the railroads to lead westward, and is later shown in the White House in 1862, signing the bill giving government support to the Union Pacific project.

The building of the two railroad lines, one from the west, the other from the east, by gangs singing "Drill, Ye Tarriers, Drill" is the chief historical feature, with a closing scene showing the driving of the golden spike in Utah, where the tracklayers met.

A love story is woven through these events, the young man, Davy Brandon, having many difficulties in his affairs with Miriam Marsh. George O'Brien, who has this leading role, is well fitted to the part, and will be noted as a comer. There will be plenty of moviegoers saying that George O'Brien's work surpasses that of J. Warren Kerrigan in The Covered Wagon, while that of Madge Bellamy as Miriam Marsh is better than that of Lois Wilson. Such comparisons are sure to be made.

We would say that as an all-around picture, The Iron Horse is as good as The Covered Wagon, measures up about equally in historical values, and is as well done.

Both picture the white-faced Hereford herds of cattle for a period when there were only longhorns roaming the ranges.   And each uses an incident from the life of Abraham Lincoln rather obscurely authenticated, so to speak.

But--the The Iron Horse, for instance, is a far, far better picture than Griffith' s America, and while not as dramatic is more accurate than The Birth of a Nation.

The Indians are rather respectable cigar store Indians, or Indians resembling those in bronze in the public parks, or those in the illustrations in picture books for children.

But the mountains, plains, wagons, horses, guns, tracks, rails, locomotives, are all the real thing, and the picture rates high as an achievement in the combination of entertainment and instruction by motion picture art.

Charles Edward Bull, not a regular movie actor at all, but, we are told, a judicial officer residing in Reno, Nev., has the role of Lincoln, and will please all who are pleased with the Borglum sculpture of Lincoln.

Sargt. Slattery and Corporal Casey are played by J. Farrell MacDonald and Francis Powers very capably.   Cyril Chadwick, Will Walling, James Marcus, Gladys Hulette, Frances Teague, and Fred Koler are members of the cast.

Buffalo Bill is played by George Wagner, Wild Bill Hickok by John Padiam, Gen. Dodge by Tex Driscoll, and Cheyenne Chief by Chief Big Tree.

John Ford directed the production and had his hands full.   The story was by Charles Kenyon and John Russell.

Two hours and twenty minutes are required for the film.   The recurring theme of the orchestra is "Drill Ye Tarriers, Drill."

Nov. 3, 1924

Josef von Sternberg

Mary Pickford's next two pictures are to be directed,

or at least the contracts so read, by Josef von Sternberg--
and the natural remark of some people is, "Whoever he is."

Sternberg was in town a day or two ago, and we had a
talk with him, or rather we listened, willing to listen, while
he talked.

His picture Salvation Hunters is to go on the screen
locally this winter, and it is a pleasure to listen to him talk-
ing about how he produced it, how much he spent for settings,
and how he believes motion pictures should be made.

In Salvation Hunters are only five players, the million
dollar settings consisted of the blue sky, the roles portrayed
are of people without the price of a ham sandwich.

This with Sternberg himself directing, also doing the
film cutting and other mechanical labors, kept the total ex-
pense of the picture, to Sternberg, down to $10,000.

And Sternberg talks about this picture as though it were
a million dollar film, yet he admits what all Hollywood knows,
that the overhead and labor outlay came to less than $10,000
cash.

Just to produce a simple little story called Salvation
Hunters.

Well, not only on the word of Sternberg, but of others,
it looks as though Douglas Fairbanks and Mary Pickford saw
the picture reeled off, and sort of went up in the air about
it.

Fairbanks offered $20,000 for a one-fourth interest in the
production, which Sternberg accepted.

And Mary Pickford said, "This is the man who must
direct my next two pictures."

We had a long talk with Josef von Sternberg, and he
seems to know more about what ought to be done in motion
picture art than anyone we have met in recent months.

That is, strictly speaking, about motion pictures as a
field and medium where the director is not just a manufacturer
producing with an eye on what the public will eat up, but
producing so that some of the most precious of the person-

ality of the director himself, as an artist, gets into the picture.

Sternberg is not quite thirty years old, and seems to be what in baseball they call a phantom.

He reminded us of Stephen Crane with his talk and his mouth, and the way he would laugh at pals without mocking at it.

And we are glad he is going to direct Mary, for Mary has slipped just a little what with Dorothy Vernon of Haddon Hall and so on.

She has just the stuff that we believe will do fine team work with von Sternberg and give us a picture worth seeing twice and then going again.

Nov. 10, 1924

Chaplin, Lloyd and Keaton

Three men are funny enough to carry comedy through seven reels--and only three so far.

Charlie Chaplin, Harold Lloyd and Buster Keaton.

All the other screen comedians have to content themselves with the two-reelers and be barrel-staved and auto-wrecked for 300 feet.

The three specified rely on specialities: Chaplin on his supreme talent as an actor, Lloyd upon novelty and Keaton upon droll "gags." When you leave a Chaplin picture you remember how great he was, when you leave a Lloyd picture you think how clever the picture was and when you leave a Buster Keaton picture you remember the jokes. In short, Chaplin makes characters, Lloyd makes situations and Keaton makes anecdotes on the screen.

Keaton's The Navigator at McVicker's this week is to the screen what musical comedy is to the stage, a series of vaudeville "gags" strung on the thin line of a story that often breaks and gets lost but which hurts nothing or nobody.

Buster takes his pessimistic mask of a face under the sea in The Navigator. He goes down in a diving suit to repair a broken propeller on a liner and wanders off in sober desperate fights with comic swordfishes and a fiery octopus. He wanders on, turning his paralyzed countenance upon cannibals who make him god of their isle and embarrass him hideously with their affection which he fears will turn into hunger at any moment.

Keaton extracts all the humor possible out of the cumbersome, unhuman diving suit and reaches what many steady moviegoers will say is the peak of his career in his new production. Kathryn McGuire, who used to wear a Mack Sennett bathing suit, is his leading lady, the girl for whom he goes on Robinson Crusoing on the bottom of the sea.

Nov. 18, 1924

Thomas Ince

The death of Thomas H. Ince removes the most consistent producer of box-office successes among all the film directors.

Where other producers had their flare-ups and their dying-downs, their good years and bad years, Ince for over a decade went ahead making pictures that made money for himself and for their showmen over America.

Filmland recognized him as its best businessman. He knew what the public wanted. He gave the public exactly that.

Art and subtle deftness of touch were things that he ignored. He knew the value of good casts, he spent lavishly on actors' salaries, he paid directors well, bought high-priced, best-selling novels to film, but the delicacies of the minds of Chaplin, Griffith and von Stroheim he laughed away as non-producers of results. The people did not appreciate fine art, he said. Why force it on them? When the time was ripe he would make that kind of picture, too.

Force, power, "punch" were his mottoes. His strident figure, his shirt-sleeved histrionics before his casts, firing them to emulate his vigor, were common sights in Hollywood.

Everything in his pictures built toward some one "walloping punch" in the story, a climax that would "knock 'em into the aisles" as Ince prayed.

The stupendous and exotic settings of De Mille were not for Ince. The extravagant photographic effects of von Stroheim he could not approve. He avoided the melancholy emotionalism of Griffith. Buoyant, strident, red-blood drama he liked and that was his output.

Occasionally he dipped into feminism for a theme, largely because one of his stars, Florence Vidor*, did not fit into the "punch" dream, but 90 per cent of his pictures went with the rattling whack of an express train going through little towns in the night.

He had a shrewd eye for potential stars. William S. Hart he discovered and with him launched a whole school of Western pictures. Charlie Ray he lifted to the stars and was engaged in lifting Ray again when he died. Charlie having come down disastrously for his own pocketbook in his attempts to star as his own management. Dorothy Dalton he turned from an extra girl into a star. Enid Bennett he brought over from Australia. Louise Glaum he discovered and lifted to a stardom that away from him she did not hold. Bessie Love he starred in the old Triangle days and brought her back after an eclipse in Those Who Dance, restoring her to the first rank again. Douglas MacLean was his find. Robert Edeson was introduced to pictures by him, also H.B. Warner and Willard Mack.

The history of motion pictures will never be written without a lot of Tom Ince in it. He is supposed to have taken more profits out of the film business than any other one man.

He knew what would go and he sent it out. It went.

Nov. 22, 1924

---

*Florence Vidor (1895-1977) had married the director King Vidor in 1915.

All Roads Lead to Valentino

A Sainted Devil is the play of the Valentino face, the
full-view, three-quarters and profile of Valentino in many
moods. The camera points at him, the art directors have
set the scenery to lead the eye to the star in every set, the
Spanish women keep their faces to him when they dance,
reach their white arms to him when they dare.

He is the landmark of every scene, and, like Rome,
all roads lead to him.

In this, his second picture since he settled his quarrels
with Paramount and returned to the screen, Rudolph Valentino
goes back to the makeup, the style, the actions that made
him a star. He returns to the Argentine and becomes again
the bad boy of the pampas and cafes as he was in The Four
Horsemen. Later on he dons a dress suit and moves among
the aristocracy of South America, but his eyes all through
are the eyes with which he looked at a savage dancer in the
second reel of The Four Horsemen and made himself thereby
a model, a style creator, a man to be imitated by the youth
of America.

At times, in this swallow-tail part of the picture,
Valentino shows a strange, weird, unhuman face, with many
of the mysteries of a Benda mask. No youth will be imitating
that.

Valentino, as he is seen now at the Roosevelt, is Don
Alonzo, a pleasant and handsome actor of ranchman wealth.
The bride his parents have brought from Spain pleases him,
but angers the ranch foreman's daughter, played with earth-
quaking venom by Nita Naldi. Don Alonzo has, it is under-
stood, taken a young aristocrat's privileges with this menial
virago, and it is to revenge this that the girl betrays the
household on the wedding night, when all the retainers are
drunk, into the hands of "El Tigre," the bandit, and his men.

El Tigre burns the hacienda, steals the bride, played
sweetly, woodenly like a Dickens heroine, by Helen D'Algy,
kills all but Don Alonzo and one follower.

Circumstances convince Don Alonzo that his wife left
willingly with the bandit, and he dedicates his life to revenge
on women and search for El Tigre.

Such a story fits the beau ideal of young America.   It
exhibits him tangoing as only Valentino can tango, toying
with feminine hearts as Valentino does in his best film way,
fighting and killing as no one expects Valentino to do.

A Sainted Devil is more Valentino than story, more
picture than sequence, but, considering that the popular in-
terest is all in Valentino and not at all in his stories, dis-
cussion of the successes and failures of this tale by Rex
Beach are idle.

The news is that Valentino is back in the Argentine.

Nov. 24, 1924

Films continued to improve in 1925, and some of the best work of the silent era was produced.

Ever inclined toward humor as well as populism, Sandburg found much to praise in both Chaplin's comedies and in such work as Erich von Stroheim's Greed; in the work of director James Cruze, another personal favorite, he found both elements, juxtaposed.

Although he had no great illusions about the worth of a reviewer's opinions, he wrote with increasing rancor of the formula picture in which the good guy lived happily ever after and the bad guy met a dingy end.

Almost unnoticed at this time, a program of three-dimensional films was screened, and a 70mm big-screen process was tried. These would not be deemed practical for some time, yet experimentation with sound continued. In 1925, William Fox installed a sound system in six of his cinemas, only to remove the equipment when public reaction proved negative. Such would not be the case for long.

Buck Jones

For a couple of years now people have been saying about Western pictures that they were all alike, that Tom Mix and Buck Jones and Hoot Gibson were good but that they needed new situations and new plots.

An Arizona Romeo relieves this condition. No person who sees this picture at the Monroe will peep about new situations for a long time, for this "Buck" Jones picture has a scene in it that is new and comic and vivid. It is that in which the heroine, a western girl who runs away from home

to marry a ranchman's son, takes a job as manicurist in a
western barbershop to while her time away waiting for the
bridegroom. With her is a friend, similarly favored by na-
ture in the way of looks, and soon in come the cowboys, the
rough and tumble buckaroos to have their nails polished. They
have never thought of so effeminate a thing before but to have
their hardened hands held in pretty girls', hours at a time,
is something new and a little bewildering. So they keep
coming back until their nails are worn to the quick and their
money gone.

Outside on the range they strive vainly to hide their
polished nails, blush furiously at the cleanliness of their fin-
gers, grow ashamed but panting at the memory of having so
charming a romance again. They suffer exquisite pangs and
saddle up and go back for more.

As it happens in Arizona Romeo it is an exceptionally
clever piece of picture making, an uproarious and true piece
of observation upon human nature.

The heroine is Sylvia Fox and the hero is Buck Jones.
Mr. Jones it is, as a chance arrival at the barbershop where
the heroine awaits her husband-to-be, who swoops off with
Miss Fox's heart.

In plot the picture is slight, suave and deft, doing what
it proposes doing with dispatch and intelligence. It never
attempts spine-chilling drama. It tries to be humorously,
honestly romantic in the western way and it is exactly that.
Mr. Jones continues to be Buck Jones, masculine, pleasant
to the eye, a genuine cowboy without undue dramatics.

Production is by William Fox and release at the Monroe
Theater.

Jan. 23, 1925

One Glorious Day

A few nights ago we saw One Glorious Day announced
at the Madison Theater, formerly the Bandbox.

Will Rogers and Lila Lee are the leading players. And
Jimmy Cruze directed the picture before he made The Cov-
ered Wagon.

The picture came out first more than a year ago, and has generally been talked about as a picture that was "too good," too intelligent, too fine to be a box-office success.

Just why this little film tale should not be a winner is hard to understand. It is a classic. The nearest we can come to giving an idea of it in a few words would be to say that it combines many of the best points of Peter Pan, of The Cabinet of Dr. Caligari and of a pleasant Dr. Jekyll and Mr. Hyde.

That may sound like a big order. But whenever colleges, schools or churches write in to this reviewer asking what would be good, clean, entertaining, instructive pictures to show to old and young, wise and foolish, we shall try to remember and put One Glorious Day on the list.

It begins with Ek. He is a spirit without a body. He wanders among the stars and the planets, and one day drops to the earth.

About the time Ek arrives a psychic professor is prom- ising an audience that at 10 o'clock the next night he will sit back in a chair in his home and his spirit shape will leave his body and come before them and speak.

And the next night it does happen. Only the professor's spirit shape is so thin that it isn't seen by the audience-- though the movie audience watching the screen sees the phan- tom. Also on this same glorious day the professor has been picked up by politicians and nominated for mayor. And Ek, electrical and dynamic, has slid into the body of the profes- sor and gone out on a wild tear. In several ways he puri- fies politics and human behavior over the town.

Will Rogers in the part of the professor is at first a doormat of a man--humble, almost sniveling. Then the transformation. The manner in which he enters a saloon and keels over the politicians and tells the world he will run independent, and the way in which he fights and conquers the large drunken brute who was making too free with a young woman--this is almost as inhuman as the running per- formances of Paavo Nurmi.*

---

*Nurmi (1897-1973) was the Finnish runner who had won seven gold medals at the 1920 Olympic Games held in Antwerp.

Then Ek finds he has worn out the body he slipped into, it isn't a tough enough material for him to go gallivanting around the earth in.   And Ek slips out and the phantom of the professor slips in.   And the professor, when he wakes up, finds himself an honored man of prowess and wisdom sure to be elected mayor, and so on.

Maybe the plot is too whimsical or maybe too scientific, edging more into the Einsteinian fields and dimensions.

Anyhow, we shall always use it among the six best photoplays we have ever seen.   And we shall thank James Cruze, the director, and Will Rogers, the leading player, for a great piece of cinema art.

Feb. 6, 1925

Salvation Hunters

Salvation Hunters, a picture having the first run in New York this month, has kicked up a good deal more than ordinary interest throughout moviedom.

First of all, it is considered this photoplay must have unusual value because Douglas Fairbanks, having had one view of it, bought a one-fifth interest in it, and because Mary Pickford, having had one view of it, decided that the maker of it must be the man to direct her in her next two pictures. And the contracts were signed.

The director, Joseph von Sternberg, is the author of the story, and on account of his wide practical experience in the mechanical and laboratory ends of the movie industry, his hand is seen in various photographic and manufacturing features of the picture.

In the list of names of the staff who worked on the film the title of "laboratory expert" is given to one.   It is recognized that after all the others have put their impress on the film there can be remarkable results achieved by the washing and manipulation of the print that is to go into the projection machines.

The story of Salvation Hunters is simple in its events

and subtle in its psychology. Three persons are lost on the
path of life, drifters down and out--a young man, a young
woman, and a child they have picked up as a mascot. They
are living on the wharves and mud scows, close to the slime
that a big steam dredge keeps digging out of the harbor bot-
tom.

The big clamshell shovel, moving, closing, opening, is
an incessant figure or symbol in the movement of the first
two-thirds of the play. It is ruthless, ironic, necessary,
hard to get away from. Finally the three vags do get away
--only to face a worse fate than any that threatened in the
harbor life.

Proffers and seductions loom before the girl. The boy
is a coward, who seems in his weak way to be pushing the
girl further toward misery. Then he wakes up. Lights
glimmer in him. Events offer him a chance to fight. And
after the fight he is a changed young man.

In photography, in lighting effects, in employment of
cheap, everyday materials for surprising and massive scenes,
the picture is masterly. We doubt whether sunshine and grass
have ever been used more effectively than in these closing
scenes, while the moving steam shovel seems to speak with
some vast, primitive vocabulary.

In the handling of the tempted drifting girl, a rarely
fine character portrait is done. One goes away haunted by
a dark, elusive struggler.

Whether the picture is destined for a popular success
is not known as yet, but that it is an achievement sure to
influence motion picture art, is a certainty. It lists among
the dozen or so of daring accomplishments that have marked
headway in motion picture art.

Feb. 14, 1925

Greed

Greed is to be to motion pictures what Theodore
Roosevelt or Woodrow Wilson were to politics--either wildly
praised or viciously condemned. Only two ways about it.
It is the best picture made to date--or the worst.

People whose temperaments are this way will laud it; people whose temperaments are that way will hate it. It is too strong to be judged with the head. No one will be rational about this picture. It will be weighed with the heart and with the emotions, and people will argue over it in the same way they argue over politics and religion.

Rumors of its strangeness, its creeping power, its eccentric composition have been sifting eastward from Hollywood for two years. Its maker, Erich von Stroheim, has been yowled at, clawed at by film and theater men who insisted that he was spending $2,000,000 of their money to make a picture that would be too realistic, too deep for the public.

To which von Stroheim replied that he had a masterpiece to work on in Frank Norris's, McTeague and that his screen version of it would be as truthful as the story itself. He said that he was working without salary on it, that he was paid for only the first six months and that he had volunteered gladly to toil for nothing during the next eighteen months in order to make his picture an epic. He told them that that fact cleared him in his own eyes and furthermore they could all go hang.

Well, it is here. The Roosevelt has it, after all these months of rumors and rampages.

Greed was written by an artist and filmed by a director who in this picture shows he is an artist. It will be remembered.

It begins with a happy marriage, a humorous, extraordinary human wedding between a hulking, slow-witted dentist and a commonplace and pretty girl of San Francisco. They set up housekeeping, then slowly, insidiously the yeast of drama begins to rise. The wife wins $5,000 in a raffle, she hides it in her bed. She begins to save on this and save on that, deny her husband carfare when he might be walking, steal dimes from his pocket at night. A former suitor in jealousy causes her husband to lose his dentist's license. The couple slips down hill as greed develops.

A tale told with skilled technique of photography, posing, and acting--von Stroheim points his camera from curious angles, intersperses the action with symbolism, varies tenement scenes with mythical, dreaming fantasy.

And he puts actors, story, cameras, settings into a soaring finale, two singed, gasping men wrecks tottering in the hot sand inferno of Death Valley.

People will love it or hate it--but they'll be a long time forgetting it either way they go on it.

Feb. 19, 1925

Among the best pictures which have come to our city within the last year--standing by itself for the low percentage of bunk and hokum--is the photoplay named Greed, now in its second week at the Roosevelt Theater.

The novel from which the story and characters are taken is a book by a great writer who came from Chicago, Frank Norris, and the name of the book is McTeague. It is about twenty-five years since McTeague was published; it is still in print and being read and there are many readers of it who place it among the greatest of American novels.

While Erich von Stroheim, the director of the picture, was working on it last year, there was plenty of skepticism about whether he could put it over.

But he did.

And he has.

Neither this country nor any other country has produced a long-range story that more ably grips the biblical text, "Money is the root of all evil," and works there from a fabric of life, with overtones or implications bordering on the allegorical.

Five thousand dollars in gold falls into the hands of a poor girl unexpectedly.

And from then on that collection of gold pieces is an actor, a sort of living player in the photodrama.

It is all that is alive in the last flicker, the final fade-out, where two men and a burro are dead in Death Valley.

What we see last of all is the pile of yellow gold pieces spotted with blood drops.

Yes, it gives some of us the shivers to look at this picture. It is as terrible as money is at its worst.

Yet we noticed through a large part of its showing that people laughed.

Some scenes and flashes and subtitles are as comic as first rate two-reel stuff.

The comedy is of the flavor of lowlife in Shakespeare.

Though the tragic high spots are fierce and relentless, the comic relief is superb.

One of the few grand instances of a movie without hokum, without a happy ending.

Feb. 23, 1925

The Genius of James Cruze

Another masterpiece can be added to the score of James Cruze. Not a masterpiece of his Hollywood or Covered Wagon mood, however, but a new and realistic masterpiece of American family life.

Cruze has done The Goose Hangs High, which ran so long and successfully on the stage of the Princess Theater last winter, and done it with humor and humanity.

Cruze is after all a sure and accurate humorist. His genius lies in making characters stand out from the film in naturalness. His own humor is an acid that eats away the backgrounds and the vague characteristics of his people and holds them forth positive and clear. The world overlooked his slips in handling the pots-and-pans life of the pioneers in The Covered Wagon, forgot his lack of realism in the matter of dirt on the people who took the dusty trail overland, waved all that aside because certain of his characters were more vividly human, gorgeously humorous than anything the camera had caught before.

Now in The Goose Hangs High Cruze deals with simple people and their complex children. It is the family and each

member of it he cares about.   The daughter may be a flapper
and the younger son a flask-carrying cake eater, but the pic-
ture is no treatise on "dangerous youth."   Cruze was inter-
ested in these two youngsters in relation to their father and
mother and grandfather, not to the world.

He ignores "problems" and the topical excitements that
cheaper directors stoop to feature.   Quite a director.   Quite
a fellow.

Constance Bennett, Edward Piel, Jr. (he was Bobby
Jones when he was younger), Esther Ralston, Myrtle Stedman
and George Irving have the principal roles.

Production is by Paramount.

March 27, 1925

The Thief of Bagdad Again

The Thief of Bagdad, which is showing at the Stratford
Theater this week, is a picture we believe has been mentioned
three or four times in this corner.

It may be nine or ten times, possibly a hundred, that
we have made reference to The Thief of Bagdad.

However many times it may be, there is no reason for
apology or explanation, because the simple fact is that The
Thief of Bagdad is one of the few pictures that ought to be
mentioned over and over.

Old and young enjoy it and derive new health from it.

In the words of the enthusiast about an all-around spring
tonic, "It's good for whatever ails you."

This reviewer has gone to see it three times and if he
lives will go again that many times more.

A wise and a foolish picture, a persuasive and sweetly
reasonable photoplay, yet also wild and impossible.

Before the city aldermen solve the traction problem they
will all have to have a look at The Thief of Bagdad.

The tax tangles at Washington would all be more easily straightened out if the members of Congress could get their throwing arms and their stiff necks loosened up by an evening with Doug Fairbanks' masterpiece.

We trust the Stratford will be packed. If our burglars, stickup men and safeblowers could all see The Thief of Bagdad they might not change their habits, but they might revise their outlooks on life.

A rare, brilliant picture that sort of wakes us up and at the same time makes us a little sleepy--a glad and mysterious picture, this one, The Thief of Bagdad.

April 20, 1925

The Last Laugh

The Last Laugh has arrived and is showing. No picture of the last year seemed to have so many people so interested that they wrote letters asking us, "Is The Last Laugh coming or has it been and gone?"

Several original and independent art features connect with this picture, which is having its first run at the Orpheum.

It is a piece of realistic story telling, that is, the people of it cut through and take hold of us like real life, though the action that in real life may take years is here compressed into a swift hour.

In front of a modern skyscraper hotel in Berlin stands the doorman; he calls the taxis and escorts guests in and out.

He is the "front" of the hotel; he wears a long proud coat with shiny big buttons on it.

The coat has become part of him; when the hotel manager notices he is too old and weak to handle the big trunks easily he is shifted to a basement job in charge of the towels and wash bowls of the lavatory.

This happens just as he is due to attend the wedding of his daughter in the tenement where everybody had regarded him as a sort of grandissimo because of his big coat with shiny buttons, which he always wore to his home.

He steals the coat; he has a gay time at the wedding.

But it is found out on him that his job is gone and the coat no longer belongs to him.

The bitterness of the downfall, as told on the screen, touches real life.

Then comes a surprise. A subtitle tells us that in life the story would so end, with the old man a sorry loser in life.

But for purposes of movie drama there is an afterpiece.

And the afterpiece is good; as epilogues go this is a hummer, the audiences enjoy it with chuckles.

Emil Jannings, who played Nero in the Quo Vadis picture, is the leading player in this; it was in The Last Laugh that he struck reputation.

May 5, 1925

While The Last Laugh is still to be seen at neighborhood theaters, we would mention that it is one of the rare and notably fine photoplays.

Those who fail to see The Last Laugh are missing one of the few screen triumphs.

It is a little sad, also it is highly intelligent, also it may not be a hundred per cent entertainment.

But it is unforgettable and has a story all its own.

The Last Laugh is one hundred per cent free from bunk.

July 20, 1925

Tom Mix Can't Act

He makes $20,000 a week.

His pictures play more theaters than do those of any other business.

His pictures play more theaters than do those of any other star, averaging 7,000 houses a picture.

He can't act, he says.

At 47 years of age he risks his neck every day. His face is known the world over.

He is Tom Mix, in many ways the most extraordinary character tossed into prominence by the movies.

His presence in Chicago to-day calls to mind the above facts about him. They are not the so-called "popular" facts about him. They are gleaned from the cold and calculating businessmen who sell films.

It has been twenty-seven years since the Spanish American War and Tom Mix was no callow fledgling then, when he rode off with the Rough Riders to follow Roosevelt through Cuba. Before that he had been a cowpuncher and a deputy sheriff. Yet today he looks no more than 30, as all the world can tell you. Daily he does for the camera athletic stunts of horsemanship that men of his age on the range abandoned twenty years ago.

Mix receives an enormous salary--really receives it, too. Twenty thousand dollars a week is a million a year and over. He gets it because he brings into the coffers of William Fox a good many times that in a year, for theater men will pay extra prices for other Fox pictures in order to get Tom Mix on their programs. Picture exhibitors just to be sure that they can show Mix engage great blocks for Fox pictures, not caring whether they are better or worse than the Mix films as attractions. Mix is what they must have.

Mix is worth that million because he makes from seven to eight to ten pictures a year, depending on the size of his productions.

He doesn't have to have vacations. As quick as he fin-
ishes one picture he starts another. He is up at work by 6
in the morning, only an hour later than he would have been
had he stayed a cowpuncher.

His recent trip to Europe was taken because his pub-
licity men wanted to let the foreigners see him in real life.
For years his pictures have booked widely in Europe.

Mix, for all his popularity across the globe, for all
his income, is freer from self-pride than almost anybody in
filmdom, big or little. He freely says he cannot act, that
he is only lucky.

Those who watch his career say that he has something
superior to classic acting in his blood--and in his pictures.
They say it is honesty. His wild western stunts are real.
He really does the things the pictures say he does. Trick
photography isn't brought onto his lot. Years of this honesty
have convinced the millions that Mix is to be trusted. And
there are a lot of worse actors in Hollywood to-day being
starred for their emotional ability, too.

Yes, quite a fellow.

May 15, 1925

The Lost World

The Lost World, which is having its first run at the
Roosevelt Theater, is a good specimen of the picture that
takes its own independent path and makes film history.

Not often do we have a photoplay that is intelligent and
exciting, that gives us science and wraps it up in a package
of adventure and love.

Out of Conan Doyle's fantastic novel they have created
a screen story that runs from a London newspaper office to
a plateau in the wilds of the Amazon River and back to London.

Wallace Beery has the best role we have ever seen him
in. He is the professor who came back from a South Ameri-
can trip with a story about immense animals of the prehistoric
period roaming a certain plateau.

Newspapers and scholars give him the laugh.

An expedition is organized to go and find and explore the region.

Bessie Love plays the role of a daughter of a scientist believed to have lost his life in the region.   Lloyd Hughes has the part of a newspaper correspondent.

The pterodactyl and brontosaurus don't sound like much when mentioned as scientific labels for animals of ten million years gone by.

The still pictures of them in books, the replicas of their forms in museums leave a good deal for the imagination.

But in this movie we see these immense creatures of former times walk and eat and creep and fly and fight so that we really believe there must have been such animals.

Many a child seeing the life portrayed here will have a good deal of the same feeling as on reading of Robinson Crusoe or the Swiss Family Robinson.

It has some of that identical loneliness and wonder.

We very positively recommend The Lost World as among the greatly conceived and greatly worked-out motion pictures.

The reels ran along an hour and forty minutes--and it's worth the time.

May 25, 1925

The most haunting photoplay production we have seen in a blue moon is this one called The Lost World.

Haunting is correct.

The blunt and lovable scientist who comes back to England with a yarn nobody believes about dinosaurs and other colossal prehistoric monsters located in a South American region--he is haunting.

The plateau where the expedition halts and finds these

monsters, on a high spot disconnected from the rest of the South American continent, the massive brontosaurus, more than a hundred feet long, and the fight of this monster with another one--this, too, haunts.

Then the return to London with a captive monster, who falls out of the steel cage in which he has been imprisoned, and who then roams the streets of the capital of the British civilization, toppling over the walls of buildings, sweeping men to death with movements of his tail and dropping through Westminster Bridge into the river--these are scenes that make a curious imprint on the memory, so that they keep coming back afterward.

We have noticed this among young people and grown-ups.

We have heard boys on the street talking about dinosaurs since this picture came.

The Lost World holds us a good deal as Robinson Crusoe.

It is for old and young and a fine specimen of what may be achieved in motion pictures when intelligence, imagination and feeling work together.

May 30, 1925

A peculiar picture from several points of view is The Lost World, the talk and the sensation of current movies.

While it is a scientific picture in the sense that it shows animals and birds of millions of years ago, animals of species that have disappeared, it is not a strictly scientific presentation because the animals seem to be alive.

They are strange, creepy, terrible animals--the brontosaurus, more than a hundred feet long with a body as bulky as a herd of elephants and a neck as slim and fancy as a giraffe--and the pterodactyl, a bird built so queer that we might think at first it was a new passenger air flivver with camouflage stuck on.

And these animals move, walk, breathe, fight, open their mouths and blink their eyes and wiggle their toes--so cunningly constructed that their movements constantly persuade they are alive.

They have been reproduced from the bones and fossils
of creatures partially reconstructed by scientists, who drew
the designs of these animals on the basis of calculations that
such animals must have lived on the earth ten million years
ago--or twelve million years ago--what's a million or two
in a case like this?

Yet this picture, The Lost World, is not so antediluvian
and sesquipedalian that it is merely for scholars and those
who want to learn science.

It interests the sport-page readers because it stages a
series of fights and hunts, spectacular conflicts of many sorts.

And it interests those who wish a love story in every
movie; this is taken care of.

And one has a mixed feeling of the comic and tragic
when the huge brontosaurus escapes from its cage in London,
terrorizes the streets of that city, sending crowds of people
in frantic flight, wandering into a museum and contemplating
the skeleton of one of its ancestors, wandering farther and
with its huge weight dropping through Westminster Bridge
into the Thames River. As a novel movie and as something
else, The Lost World is to be recommended.

June 6, 1925

Griffith, Fields and Sally of the Sawdust

The new Griffith picture at the Roosevelt Theater, Sally
of the Sawdust, stands in a class by itself, so far as Griffith
himself is concerned.

For years this important originator in photoplay art has
been an independent operator, going on his own.

But being artist and manager both was too much work
and worry, and he has begun work on a salary for the Famous
Players-Lasky Corporation.

And while making Sally of the Sawdust he remarked
something like, "This is the first picture I have made in ten
years where I didn't have a megaphone in one hand and a
mortgage in the other."

Well, this <u>Sally</u> picture is good, standing away up among the best of the year.

And some will say it is the best Griffith has done since he made <u>Broken Blossoms.</u>

Carol Dempster plays Sally, and this is the most insinuating and implicative work the silversheet has seen of her lithe, swift, straightaway art.

If your heart enjoys that twist of the byway of life where tears and laughter come close to mixing, where pain turns with jokes at itself, and the terms of tragedy and comedy get lost like sunshine and rain during a sunshower, then take a look at Miss Dempster playing Sally, unaccountably merging monkeyshines and majesty.

Sometimes it is an elusive personality and sometimes a deliberate accomplished art of pantomime that stands forth in Miss Dempster's portrayal of Sally, so that she creates great moments--one has to pause and consider whether any recent cinema playing compares with hers.

W. C. Fields as Prof. Eustace McGargle, spieler, faker and three-card man, is also a new development.

In some of the scenes we note that Griffith still keeps his hand; he has superb qualities and maintains his leadership among the entertainers who achieve something more than entertainment.

Besides circus and carnival people there are highly respectable persons presented as the story goes.

Besides bootleggers and peanut vendors and acrobats, there are detectives and hypocrites, the goulash of civilization.

Alfred Lunt and Effie Shannon have roles, also Erville Anderson and Glenn Anders; also Charles Hammond and Roy Appleseed.

We recommend <u>Sally of the Sawdust</u> as entertainment, a blend of misery and monkeyshines, and majesty.

July 21, 1925

And now comes the much ridiculed "brown derby" into its own!

Charlie Chaplin immortalized the black derby; Harry Langdon the flat and funny "lid," Raymond Griffith* the high silk hat, Lloyd Hamilton** the checkered cap!

W.C. Fields--who springs to screen comedian fame in D.W. Griffith's Sally of the Sawdust at the Roosevelt--has begun to make the "brown derby" famous.   Fields has been making the multitudes roar for years as chief comic of Ziegfeld Follies.   Now, the camera has caught him and his first big picture proves that his comedy can be put across on the screen even more uproariously than on the stage.   His antics with the "brown derby" created laugh after laugh.   As the circus juggler, side-show barker, card-sharper, shell-game manipulator, Fields wears the brown derby naturally.   His only other means of comedy are a cane (à la Chaplin) and a cigar stump.   Undoubtedly, Fields had much to do in helping D.W. Griffith make Sally of the Sawdust the laugh-hit that it is.

July 22, 1925

The Ten Commandments

While The Ten Commandments is showing this week at the Castle and Senate theaters, it might perhaps be well to take note that this is one of the few pictures that actually ran up and over $1,000,000 in cost.

It is well conceded that by the time the Israelites had crossed the Red Sea and the Egyptians in pursuit were flooded over and destroyed and annihilated and obliterated, the picture was well started on its $1,000,000 expense account.

And there was yet the big fake concrete skyscraper to

---

*Griffith (1894-1937) was a prolific comedian but often remembered for his serious role in All Quiet on the Western Front (1930).

**Hamilton (1893-1935) had been one half the comedy team of Ham and Bud, with Bud Duncan.

erect, besides all the time parties, dinners, and clothes, gowns, garbs and apparelings of the sort Cecil De Mille finds necessary for a picture.

In this connection, that of the $1,000,000 cost, we were told by one whom we consider an authority, "When it was finished The Ten Commandments would have to gross over $3,000,000 at the box office in order to pay for its first cost of $1,200,000."

And it was partly in connection with the failure of the picture to approximate this $3,000,000 that Cecil De Mille became involved in differences of opinion at the Famous Player-Lasky headquarters, where he had the title of "Director General."

And where Cecil De Mille used to be the accredited high man of the directors of Famous Players-Lasky, he is now on the outside of that organization, and for six months has been at the head of various producing units from whom, month-by-month, pictures have been expected but have not been forthcoming, at the offices of the Producers' Distributing Corporation.

The Ten Commandments is a strange production from many angles.

It is Cecil De Mille's masterpiece; he put into it everything he knew about showmanship and what is called hokum; the old homestead and the religious mother with one boy who is good and slow and another boy who is bad and fast; she reads the Bible to them and the panorama of the Red Sea is unfolded; then comes the action wherein the good boy who is slow triumphs over the bad boy who is fast.

We were interested to hear the comment of a member of the general board of the Presbyterian Church, who teaches the largest Sunday School class in the city of St. Paul. He said, "When I saw the first of this photoplay I said to myself I would like to show it to my Sunday School class. But when I saw the second half I said it wouldn't do."

Leatrice Joy, L. Rod La Roque, and Nita Naldi got their starts to stardom in this picture.

Will Rogers makes the comment that while Jeanie

MacPherson is credited with the scenario, the best part of it is from Exodus, by a famous ancient author.

Aug. 4, 1925

Chaplin's The Gold Rush

In The Gold Rush, our old college chum Charlie Chaplin has accomplished two things.

He makes use of his old-time laugh-making stunts-- with a swifter twist to them.

And then he has interwoven serious things not to be found at all in his old-time films.

From some angles The Gold Rush is an epic in the sense that Frank Norris's novels, McTeague and The Octopus, were epic.

Just as a piece of story telling it is immense.

We can name, if required, a printer, a professor, a photographer, a lawyer and a newspaper man who have been to see the picture twice and have viewed it from start to finish three times.

Of all the pictures Chaplin has made this seems to have more of a pull on it to "come see me again" than any other he has made.

A New York friend tells us Charlie had a string of dinner engagements fixed up for him there; he fixed up one or two of them himself.

And then he didn't show up at a single dinner.

They knew, of course, that he wasn't hungry.

And they tried to figure out what had happened.

As near as they could spell out the cabalistic signs of the mystic diagram, Charlie eats when he pleases--just as he makes pictures and hands them out to the great, hungry public when he pleases.

He is an independent artist forty ways.

If he arrives to-day on the Twentieth Century as scheduled, he will be looked at a little more than hitherto--on account of The Gold Rush.

Aug. 21, 1925

To see Charlie Chaplin eat his Thanksgiving dinner of boiled "sole" is alone worth the price of admission to The Gold Rush, his latest and truthfully heralded "best" photo-play, having its premiere at the Orpheum Theater this week. Mr. Chaplin wrote the play, directed it, and has made it a literal scream by his own inimitable acting.

The Gold Rush deals with the adventures of a lone pros-pector (Charlie Chaplin) caught by the gold fever of 1898. He fares optimistically forth to conquer the North with the inevitable Chaplin hat and cane, plus a blanket. He is storm-swept into the cabin of Black Larson--desperado. Big Jim Mackay--who has just "staked" a mountain of gold--blows in too, and then the fun begins. It wouldn't be fair to give it all away here. There is, of course, a girl and such fight-ing as always occurs in places where "men are men," but when Charlie, the tramp, suddenly turns multimillionaire, Mr. Chaplin displays real artistry. A final hint--with winter coming on and all that--ambitious money-makers can profit well by Charlie's lesson in snow-shoveling.

Come again, Mr. Chaplin.

Aug. 25, 1925

Wild Horse Mesa

This Wild Horse Mesa picture, having its first run at McVicker's Theater this week, has its Chief credit, we sup-pose, to Zane Grey, the novelist.

It is from his book that the desert, the buffalo, the steers, the roaming, raving, raging horses are derived.

The barbwire--we nearly forgot to say that barbwire figures big.

In the cast for this movie they should include, perhaps, Barbwire, and Wild Horses.

An exciting wild melodrama, this is. It tells the truth about the desert, about desert people and horses and desert life in general.

And then it goes on piling up one thing on another, one melodramatic coincidence slipped on top of another until after a while it is telling more than the truth, so much more than the truth, the whole truth and nothing but the truth, that it fools those who take it as the truth until they know less about the desert than if they had never heard of Zane Grey.

And such a picture as Wild Hose Mesa is worth seeing if it is taken as melodrama, as half truth, as fact set raging and raving.

Jack Holt and Noah Beery are seen, one as a perfectly good man, without fault, flaw or blemish, while the other is a perfectly bad man, sneeringly fiendish through and through, beyond hope of redemption.

And the good man lives, triumphs and fulfills his dreams, while the bad man dies the driveling death of a discredited dirty dog.

All of which is the customary and regular and accepted thing in a Zane Grey novel or picture.

The heroine, Sue Melburne, played by Billy Dove, is grammatical and tender-hearted, and a peculiarly regular wild flower desert of Zane Grey make and manufacture.

Little Doug Fairbanks, Jr. is worth seeing.

George B. Seitz directed the picture.

Sept. 3, 1925

The Phantom of the Opera

The Phantom of the Opera gives a new meaning to the

word "sensational." Universal's new production seeks for the chilling thrill, the scene that scares you, which is yet so new, so fascinating that your pleasure surpasses your scare. Its climax creeps upon you by compelling degrees; you shrink from it, yet you would not miss it.

Reel after reel speeds by and you sit on your chair edge waiting, waiting for the climax, which is to be the unmasking of the strange "phantom." Through crowds, lonely streets, tunnels, spooky corridors and gala throngs this "phantom" stalks. Detectives follow him, walls open to him, he is here, there, and then neither here nor there, always with his mask. A girl worships him, a hero hates him, mobs hunt him, still he hides behind a bland, smooth, horrible, vacant, false face. Sometime he is going to toss it off and show you just what it is he's hiding--and you wait for that "sometime" --terribly fascinated, aching with suspense.

He sits at an organ, this "phantom" deep down in the subterranean caverns beneath the Opera House of Paris, looking through his bland and innocent and mysterious mask at the keys over which his fingers run. Behind him on a deep divan, swathed in silks, is the girl he has taught to sing so well that she has conquered all Paris. Behind her, still further, is the magnificent room where the phantom sleeps-- in a coffin. Above, the hunt for them goes on. A frantic lover, a dogged detective, and a mob of outraged stagehands from the Opera are hunting the phantom who has made the girl opera star and stolen her after terrorizing the audience, with switching lights off and on, with terrible threats and acts.

The great moment is at hand. The girl can stand the suspense no longer. Neither can you. She has been warned never to lift the mask. But now when he is intent on his music, she comes closer, closer, her fingers steal toward the ribbon that fastens the mask. Her fingers give one final twitch--and there you are!

You may squeak out loud with excitement, but you'll stay in the theater, for with that the action grows swifter and carries you on with it. But you'll never forget that one indescribable moment when your eyes are creeping, creeping toward the ribbon that fastens on the mask, creeping with the frightened fingers of the girl.

The Phantom of the Opera gives Lon Chaney another

fantastic makeup--one that resembles Chaney not at all, re-
sembles nothing you ever saw or will see again. That is a
tribute to his makeup and to the versatility of his acting: a
genuine artist, Mr. Chaney.

Mary Philbin and Norman Kerry are the lovers. Arthur
Carew, the mysterious detective. The mobs are led stri-
dently and splendidly by Gibson Gowland and the scenery is
mountainous, its settings partly in color. Rupert Julian di-
rected the picture and its current release is at the Roosevelt
Theater.

Dec. 7, 1925

Rin-Tin-Tin

Rin-Tin-Tin, the phenomenal Belgian police dog whose
intelligence as well as whose beauty have brought him into
fame as one of the most popular motion-picture stars, is at
the State-Lake Theater this week in the latest and one of the
best of his pictures. It is entitled The Clash of the Wolves
and in it Rin-Tin-Tin rises to heights of intelligence which
even he has never before revealed.

When Rin-Tin-Tin swept the country with Where the
North Begins, it seemed unlikely that the success of that
picture could be repeated with any degree of frequency, be-
cause pictures were not made every day that afforded real
opportunities to stars, especially when those stars happen to
be dogs. The marvelous "Rinty" seemed fated from the start
to be a flash in the pan, not for lack of talent, but for lack
of material.

However, Warner Bros., the producers who first rec-
ognized the dog's starring possibilities, have so far been
consistently successful in obtaining stories that not only give
Rin-Tin-Tin his chance, but stories that stand up on their
own account as first-rate screen material.

So far the Rin-Tin-Tin pictures have included Where
the North Begins, Find Your Man, The Lighthouse by the
Sea, Tracked in the Snow Country and Below the Line, an
unbroken string of successes. Now there can be added to
the list, The Clash of the Wolves, which in many ways
seems to be the most stimulating of the lot.

The scene is laid in the Southwest cattle country, and the swift action moves against a background of burning beauty. There are gorgeous views of the Painted Desert, and a thrilling spectacle is the sight of a forest fire in the High Sierras.

This fire gives a start to a story that rages and blazes and flames with drama. The fire drives a fierce pack of wolves out from the forest down into the cattle lands, ravaging and marauding as they go. Their leader is "Lobo," the role played by Rin-Tin-Tin. Wounded, he is cared for by a lone prospector, and the prospector's love for his outlaw pet leads to dramatic complications that are alive with suspense and excitement.

Rin-Tin-Tin, as the wolf, is thrillingly intelligent in reflecting a wide gamut of emotions. A beautiful animal, he has a power of expression in his every movement that makes him one of the leading pantomimists of the screen. In the new picture he introduces a comedy element that is likely to confound those who imagine animals have no sense of humor.

June Marlowe, who has been the dog's leading lady on a number of other occasions, again lends her soulful beauty to the role of the heroine, and Charles Farrell, a handsome newcomer among leading men, makes a sincere and attractive hero. Heinie Conklin, the veteran vaudeville headliner, supplies some joyous comedy relief, and the heavy villainies are well attended to by Pat Hartigan.

The picture was written by Charles A. Logue and directed by Noel Smith.

Dec. 15, 1925

Movies Have Never Been Better

Americans are at last beginning to make motion pictures their own. Film productions are changing to a style more typically American, getting more humorous and less comic, more dry and droll and less fevered.

Old World heaviness of emotions and a primitive earnestness of drama have ruled motion pictures up till now. The average program picture has been a mixture of desperately

serious passion and burlesque comedy. They have been highly
serious stories interlarded with "gags" and joke situations,
sprinkled in with an eye to the box office rather than fitness
in the story.

But of late motion pictures have been doing what used
to be thought impossible, making successes out of wit and
humor themes, telling stories of people's characters rather
than of their adventures. These bear no relation at all to the
two-reel comedies, just as Charlie Chaplin's Gold Rush, for
all its baggy trousers and grotesqueries, was totally unlike the
racing two-reelers with which the unthoughtful class it. The
Gold Rush was a masterpiece, not for the laughter it caused,
but for the interest it created in its chief character, the for-
lorn little "bum" whose hopes and humiliations, through Chaplin's
genius, became absorbing to audiences.

The same thing may be said of Adolphe Menjou. He is
making pictures of humorous characterization and is, thereby,
a star. Polished, subtle, witty, he makes his roles amusing,
delightful, immensely tickling, without a single tumble or loss
of wearing apparel. His The King on Main Street is said by
eastern critics to be something highly original in this line.

The enormous success of Constance Talmadge's Her Sis-
ter from Paris across the country is another instance of the
point. Wholly facetious and hilarious, it relies on situations
and predicaments for its laughter, not on a single clownish
action.

Raymond Griffith and Johnny Hines are attempting more
and more intelligent humor and less and less funny falls for
their full-length comedies, and are succeeding. First National
has even gone so far as to put Corinne Griffith in a "wise-
cracking" pert story of Edna Ferber's Classified, wherein she
is a "wise" and self-confident working girl whose smart an-
swers and unsentimental mind eventually lead her to discard
a handsome millionaire and wed a slangy garagekeeper, with
whom she has a chance to live happily ever after.

John Gilbert, in The Merry Widow, exhibits rare humor
whenever he has a chance, exactly the sort of thing American
filmgoers are clamoring for. In a drunken scene he throws
tradition to the wind and is drunk to the life, caring nothing
for heroism or posing.

The wind is blowing a healthy lack of sentimentalism in

pictures, a strong, lusty sense of humor that is one with American life.

Dec. 24, 1925

Hollywood had another outstanding year, and so did Sandburg, whose literary aspirations got a big boost with publication of both his two-volume Abraham Lincoln: The Prairie Years and his Selected Poems, edited by Rebecca West. All the while, his film appetite was increasingly being satisfied by the variety of excellent movies.

Although the death of Valentino, at the time of his last and most substantial film, Son of the Sheik, created a sensation, Sandburg was more taken with large-scale movies with good production values: Variety, Ben Hur, Phantom of the Opera, and What Price Glory. He also laughed at Harold Lloyd, and took more than passing note of a process called Vitaphone, first used in August for the movie Don Juan. That film, the first feature with synchronized music and effects, called for the film projector to be linked mechanically to sound discs. Although Vitaphone was ultimately discarded in favor of sound recorded visually beside the film image, it was the first serious attempt to win public support for sound. As such, it was to be both a clarion call to competitors and a death knell for the silents.

The Novelty of The Phantom of the Opera

Sometimes when we don't know what else to say about a production, we remark, "It's a novelty, anyhow."

And The Phantom of the Opera, having its run at the Castle Theater this week, is strictly among the novelties of the season.

The movie goers who have a good time telling each other through the opening reels just how the story is going to come out in the last reels can't have their customary satisfaction. An old-fashioned terror and mystery story of the French school, and by a French writer, is done here in a clever manner worth the study of psychologists of public taste.

The aim is to send cold shivers registering down the spines of the members of the audience.

But these cold shivers must not be ice cold, must not go so far as they did in The Cabinet of Dr. Caligari.

Nor as they did in Erich von Stroheim's Greed, which pictured Frank Norris' novel, McTeague.

The latter two movies were not very strict box-office successes, they were too fierce.

In making The Phantom of the Opera they figured on scaring the audience--but not too much, not too fierce.

The phantom public wants its phantoms on the screen, but these phantoms musn't be phantasmagoric.

Lon Chaney's best acting, with his hands, is to be seen in this picture. He wears a grisly mask most of the time and therefore the talking must be done with his hands, or the shoulders, or feet. And he does very well with hands and shoulders.

And wisely leaves Charlie Chaplin as the unchallenged champion of speech with the feet.

Jan. 11, 1926

Ben Hur

The picturization of Ben Hur, A Tale of the Christ by Gen. Lew Wallace will occupy the stage of the Woods Theater beginning this evening and twice daily hereafter. New York, Boston, Chicago and Philadelphia are the only cities which will see the epic this season. First, a word of history to the younger generation. Ben Hur was put forth by Gen. Lew

Wallace in 1880, and for 45 years the book enjoyed a circulation second only to Holy Writ.

It is a tale that weaves intimately the founding of Christianity into the environment and lives of the characters, the young Ben Hur being pictured as a contemporary of the Savior. A beautiful romance links the Jewish prince and Esther, the daughter of his steward Simonides.

The story begins in Bethlehem with the star and the adoration of the wise men, then deals with the oppression of Judea and the ruin of the Hur family by Roman edict. The hero is successively a slave in the galleys, then by turn of fortune, a Roman duumvir's adopted son, the richest subject in Asia, winner of the Antioch chariot race, and then animated by the Jewish idea of a temporal messiah he raises a legion to take up arms for Jesus of Nazareth. But the Prince of Peace comes not into a worldly kingdom. Ben Hur is bidden to put up his sword, becoming a humble follower of the Master. His long lost mother and sister are restored to him and are cured of sickness by the divine healing.

For nearly a quarter of a century from November 29, 1899, the stage play of Ben Hur, founded on the above story, was the most popular stage attraction in America. This has been succeeded in turn by the Metro-Goldwyn-Mayer motion picture, which was begun in 1923 and completed December, 1925. Abraham L. Erlanger* has seen to it that the new Ben Hur is a faithful picturization of the book and play, but with the immensely grander resources of the motion picture art, especially in the sea fight and chariot race. Ramon Novarro heads the cast of 100,000 players. Metro-Goldwyn-Mayer have expended $4,000,000 on the picture.

Feb. 8, 1926

An Unspectacular Spectacle

The Wanderer, well, The Wanderer is what it is.

---

*Erlanger (1860-1930) was owner of an important theater chain who earlier had originated the idea of a central clearing house for touring attractions. A figure of great wealth and power, he was known as "the Little Napoleon" of the theatrical world.

Some will say it is a loud racket in the silent drama.

Others will hold that it tries to babble in the Babylonian tongue and says nothing, having nothing to say.

As a spectacle picture it is nothing to put your spectacles on and look at if you have hitherto seen one or two of the so called spectacle pictures.

What if a thing does cost $1,000,000 and is very umptyump spectacular and then those that produced it didn't care very much about it, didn't love it and didn't dream about it while they were making it?

This is it or very much just that kind of a photoplay.

If any earnest Hyde Park Bible students should come as a committee asking this reviewer's advice as to what photoplays would be good for their Bible classes, we would say this is third rate.

We are sure that Ernest Torrance and Wallace Beery could do some first-class work as dramatic interpreters of the scriptures in the pantomime medium if they had half a chance. If given a story and collateral characters and a cast that didn't most of the time look like a little from George White's Scandals, and a little more from any of the other recent skirtless stage productions. They aimed at joy and we got monotony.

Story? Jether, played by William Collier, Jr., is shepherding in the hills, and Tisha, priestess to the false god, Tehlar, passes and is struck with the beauty of the boy, as the subtitles say, and instructs Tola, her servant, to beguile the boy back to the big city where she can get at him.

Which Tola does.

Then everything is very Babylonian and fleshly.

The fleshpots are chaotically full and running over.

It gets monotonous and we've seen it before in many and many a movie.

Then a prophet appears, foreordaining the doom of the revelers.

Forked lightning and rain of fire and earthquakes tumble the walls and it is a holocaust of a holiday or so they mean it to be, though it is actually about as impressive as any angry child kicking over a house of blocks.

After it's all over and the prodigal son has no longer a big city to play in he harks back home to again be a little shepherd in the hills, among the open spaces where men are men and the woodbine twineth.

Greta Nisson had poor direction or rusty direction; so did Tyrone Power and the whole cast.

We wonder how Raoul Walsh, the director, takes the banter of his friends about this.

He probably answers he set out to outdo Cecil De Mille and kicked up nearly as much excitement as The Ten Commandments without spending a quarter of the money.

This is one of the Paramount pictures, offered for the whole family, but the children might as well stay at home with any rotogravure section.

Feb. 16, 1926

Guessing What the Public Wants

What would you do if you were Fox, Laemmle, Zukor, Lasky or any of the big bosses of the western picture business?

You would have on your hands a production plant costing millions of dollars, and the question you would be asking yourself would be, "What kind of pictures must I produce so that I can pay other people salaries, wages, royalties, insurance, upkeep, depreciation, and after that pay myself a profit?"

You would either ask that question and answer it properly or else go out of business.

The production of motion pictures is first of all a business, an industry, and only secondarily, an art.

More than 20,000,000 American people a day go to the movies.

An immense establishment is guessing all the time as to what this moviegoing public wants.

The habit has them.   They want what they want when they want it.

They will stop going when they say, "I'm tired of the movies."

Sometimes the whole works at Hollywood and in New York is guessing wrong on some points.

A while ago they were saying, "The people don't want war pictures, they are sick of the war."

Then came Laurence Stallings with The Big Parade, now at the Garrick Theater.

And then followed Behind the Front, and, it seems, a little flock of war pictures.

So all the time they are wondering what to guess next.

April 4, 1926

Movies in a Hurry

The comment is often heard that a good many movies seem to be made in a hurry.

Directors, photographers and players have their eyes on a clock and a release date as they swiftly peg along aiming to get the film out of the factory in time for shipment to this or that theater where the patrons are standing in a line a half block long waiting for the new show.

Often in this corner we have mentioned how this or that picture struck us.

What struck us most about it was that it was slapdash.

It had been hustled through an inexorable process with one eye on the time sheets.

They didn't have time to care for it or put in the little touches or to honestly humanize it.

Sometimes we believe we went a little too far in registering this point about the new releases.

Our conscience had faint, flickering twinges.

It couldn't be called remorse, but it edged onto regret and dubious viewpoints.

Therefore, we were cheered up and felt better to-day on looking through our old friend, the Film Daily, which calls itself and comes close to being "the recognized authority."

We read two jokes. No. 1 was like this:

A director of western films had lingered over his luncheon longer than he should have. Glancing at his watch he remarked:

"Well, it's 2:30. Just time to get back to the studio and shoot another western before the day ends."

And no. 2:

First Magnate--"Yes, sir I intend building thirty first runs all over the country on the two-a-day basis."

Second Magnate--"That's interesting. Let me see, that will take you just fifteen days, won't it?"

April 22, 1926

For Heaven's Sake

There is an aged pastor who cannot fill his rescue mission. Not even the presence of his beautiful daughter will attract bums and hoboes to salvation. It is a situation calculated to touch the boob heart Harold Lloyd displays chronically upon the screen. So Harold, peering brightly through his tortoise shells upon a slum world, goes out to drum up a crowd.

He insults street loafers and teases them into chasing

him, he upsets apple carts and draws the yowling owners into the pursuit, he slaps dozing yeggs and provokes them to join the hunt. He covers the lowlands of a great city, tempting its scum to rise up and kill him, and when a backward glance tells him that he has a crowd sufficiently large, he upsets enough policemen to follow and leads the whole crew into the mission where he assumes the prayer book and convinces the maddened underdogs that the only way they can avoid merited arrest is to pray and sing. The police are baffled and stand gaping while cutthroats and thugs chant "Brighten the Corner."

That is the start of Harold Lloyd's new feature-length comedy, For Heaven's Sake, at the Roosevelt.

And from that point the fun may be said to begin. From there on the thugs embrace the wealthy and society youth as their own little pal, and he is kept busy holding them to an uncomfortable obedience to the law while he woos the pastor's pretty daughter.

Three grotesque yeggs, in particular, adopt him, and, in preparation for his wedding to the girl, get howling drunk and swamp him with endearments.

One of them, by way of incident, bumps into a stuffed bear outside a taxidermist shop and wheeling savagely, focuses bleary eyes on the animal, saying "Take off that coat and fight."

Mr. Lloyd's little pals are all over town and rounding them up he commandeers a motor bus for safe passage home.

It is the careening career of this bus through thickest Los Angeles that gives the picture its highest humor and thrill. At an apparent fifty miles per hour the bus, now driverless, now guided by many drunken hands, topples on the edges of viaducts, razors past baby buggies, shaves automobiles, just misses express trains and draws shivering squeaks of excitement out of the staidest burghers who throng the Roosevelt.

As a stunt this bus ride is the stuntiest that Harold has had since he hung by his eye-winkers from the skyscraper in Safety Last. It keeps him in his unique place on the screen, not so important an actor as Charles Spencer Chaplin by any stretch of the imagination, but the best showman the comic spirit has had to date on the screen.

April 9, 1926

Harold Lloyd's latest picture, For Heaven's Sake, has much headwork and understanding of human nature back of it.

Though we may go saying, "We have seen Harold in so many pictures we doubt whether he can spring anything new on us."

But the organization working with and for Harold got their skypieces working, their noodles, their think tanks.

And the result is a concatenation of devices, exploits and nut notions that reach out from the screen and keep the audience bubbling with innocent mirth.

On the day we see this we should eat no nut sundae because this is enough for a day.

Or it may be that the nut sundae is to be drunken and not eaten.

Or it may be that the nut sundae is our chief national invention of a commodity that is a liquid bun and therefore neither a drink nor a sandwich but a mystery.

All this may sound a little mixed like a mixture, but it is not so much of a mixture as For Heaven's Sake, one of the cleverest decoctions we have seen from the headache town of Hollywood.

What they do in this movie they couldn't get away with if they did it slow.

Things happen so silly that if we had time to think 'em over we would walk out on the show.

But each silly flash is so swiftly followed by another, each fitted into the other like the sections of a revolving door, that the first thing we know we have seen another movie and when we ask ourselves what it was all about, it seems as though we are trying to think of a long string of jokes in any old almanac.

As movie comedies go, the batting average of For Heaven's Sake is high and its wisdom is on the order of Moss asking Fry, "How high is up?"

April 12, 1926

Valentino in Son of the Sheik

The comeback of Rudolph Valentino in Son of the Sheik is all that can be asked for by those who were accustomed at one time to rank him highest, those who first gave him that nickname of "the great lover."

It was The Four Horsemen and The Sheik that put him on the map.

And now in Son of the Sheik he does everything that he did in The Sheik only with more restraint and decency.

But in this latest film he plays two parts, that of a sheik and the son of a sheik.

It is having its first run at the Roosevelt Theater this week and seems to be giving pleasure to the patrons thereof.

Vilma Banky is the leading lady, playing a dancing girl who wins the son of the sheik, against the wishes of the iron-willed father.

Then she loses her sheik.

But wins him again.

'Tis a movie.

Miss Banky is excellent as the dancing girl who loves, hates, and loves.

Mr. Valentino is excellent as sufferer, as rescuer, as rider, as the handsome male of the desert sands who will brook no disturbance of his peace of soul.

Karl Dane is excellent, not quite so excellent as when he excelled as Slim in The Big Parade, but considering his Arabian clothes, the rags around his head, and so on, pretty good at that.

George Fawcett, Bull Montana, Agnes Ayres and Montague Love are other stars of a starry cast.

George Fitzmaurice directed and must have had his

megaphone filled with sands of the desert along the Pacific Coast dunes several times.

July 30, 1926

Valentino's Appeal to Women

Rudolph Valentino's wide popularity, which this week is seen to have been a more amazing fame in extent than was at first supposed, traces back to a number of causes*.

Rudy was the center of a romance of wealth, for one thing. In his earlier days on the screen he was referred to by rivals and envious commentators as "the dishwasher."

It may be that some people now as they pass a restaurant sign "Dishwasher Wanted" will pause to say: "Well, the one they get may rise--Valentino did."

Then, too, he embodied in a picturesque way something of sudden romance, of money not counted in tens of thousands or hundreds of thousands, as the best of stage stars count it, but in millions. "Rudy? Oh, he made a million last year."

Then there was the gossip about him, there was his adventuring, changing, shifting, hunting for the woman he wanted, his first divorce that wasn't a divorce, so that he had to annul a marriage. And after that the woman whom he married, unmarried and remarried, finally had to be divorced. And while he was hinting that he had temperament and never would find the woman he wanted, a dark-haired Polish screen actress was announcing that he and she were betrothed.

Thus he was kept in the minds of people, many people. His actual screen audience may not have equaled that of Tommy Meighan; it certainly was not as large as that of Harold Lloyd. But Rudy called somehow to that vague, intangible thing called romance. A touch of the exquisite, carried sometimes to extravagance, clung about him; no statistician can inform us how far he provoked or furthered the young male custom of slicking back the hair in what is called "the young sheik style."

---
*Valentino had died a few days earier, on August 23, 1926.

He appealed to a wide audience of men and women, boys
and girls, but chiefly women and girls, as having grace and
personal charm. If they read stories saying, "The young
prince was of comely features and a surprising bodily grace,"
their first thought on trying to fix such a type in real life
was of Rudolph Valentino.

Aug. 28, 1926

Valentino and Kisses to Stardom

Alice Terry is the first of a long list of girls whom
Rudolph Valentino "kissed into stardom."

She was the first actress to share the romantic popular-
ity of Rudy, for it was she whom he kissed so ardently and
incomparably in The Four Horsemen. Immediately she was
signed for stardom, just as girl after girl after girl in film-
dom was singled out for large contracts after Valentino had
kissed them on the screen. One remembers this seeing her
in Mare Nostrum at the Roosevelt.

The list is long. Agnes Ayres, who had fallen from
stardom and who had been seen but little on the screen, was
selected by him for The Sheik, and after that picture had
flamed across the country Agnes was a star again. Rudy's
kisses had brought her good luck. Then there was Helen
D'Algy, totally unknown, who was Rudy's heroine in The
Sainted Sinner. He kissed her and Metro-Goldwyn-Mayer
signed her. Doris Kenyon had failed as a screen star and
was back on the stage when Valentino asked her to play op-
posite him in Monsieur Beaucaire. He gave her a kiss just
before the Booth Tarkington romance ended and First National
dashed on the scene to sign her for stardom. Nita Naldi had
been an "extra girl" or player of minor parts before Rudy
selected her to play the vampire who ruins the bullfighting
hero with a kiss in Blood and Sand. After that Paramount
gave her featured roles and her salary soared. Vilma Banky
had never "gone over" as a star and was about to be shipped
back to Vienna, whence she had come, until Valentino took
her and kissed her in The Eagle. With him she "found her-
self." Now, after Son of the Sheik, she is a star herself.

He kissed them into stardom; his own romance lent

itself to others.   Many of the girls did not have the talent
to succeed after he had set them on the path to greatness.
Most of them have disappeared from the screen.   Alice
Terry in <u>Mare Nostrum</u>, now at the Roosevelt, comes near-
est to matching him.

Aug. 30, 1926

Corinne Griffith

If there ever was a girl in motion pictures who was un-
deniably an aristocrat in bearing it is Corinne Griffith.   No
actress has, in manner, so unquestionable a patrician up-
bringing.   Her movements, her delicate beauty, all have the
stamp of expensive girls' schools and Parisian tutors and
long, long trips on the continent.

Which is all a great and ironic joke on those character
analysts who tell what people have been, or are, by looking
at their faces.

For Corinne Griffith was a waitress in a Texas town
and it took a bit of argument by King Vidor and his then wife,
Florence, to get Corinne to quit shouldering trays and go west
for to be a movie actress.

"The orchid of the screen," they call her now, and she's
become sort of a dream heroine of films, the lovely lady of
the ivory towers.

Lately Corinne has had an idea she was getting too much
that way, too dreamlike, and she's been jazzing it up, playing
<u>Classified</u> and <u>Mlle. Modiste</u>, where slang and pep and
wisecracks were thick and fast.

She's turned away from her regal triumphs and worked
back into shopgirl roles.   And even when she started to make
<u>Into Her Kingdom</u>, which now unreels at the Chicago Theater,
and was faced with the task of playing a czarist grand duchess
in robes and sandals and Siberian sentences of doom, she
couldn't let it go at that.   She twisted the plot happily so that
the heroine comes to New York as a refugee and goes to work
in a drygoods store as a simple little clerk.

Corinne is her old self, the exquisite lady of loveliness
in the czarist scenes, haughty, imperious, languishing of
manner, but she is her new self, her real self, the waitress
with deft, sure talents of acting, when she gets behind the
counter.

Into Her Kingdom is, as a story, an interesting example
of the way people make up myths about kings and leaders who
disappear mysteriously. It pretends that the czar's second
daughter, the Grand Duchess Tatiana, wasn't killed with her
folks by the bolsheviki that morning years ago now, but that
she got away with a peasant, Stephan, to America, and that
when the imperialists came to take her back for a coup rebel-
lion and restoration of the Romanoffs she took her baby in
her arms and looked past the kneeling royalists out the window
of her Brooklyn flat and said, "I am not Tatiana."

It may be in time that this piece of fiction will pass
into legend and be believed, just as millions now believe the
little dauphin of France was spirited away from revolution-
aries and lived and died in North America.

Aug. 3, 1926

Vitaphone Demonstrated

The first presentation locally of a motion picture play
with a mechanically synchronized orchestral accompaniment
took place last night at McVicker's Theater when Warner
Brothers put on their Vitaphone show.

The picture play was Don Juan with John Barrymore
starring, with Willard Louis as the male comic, Mary Astor
as the leading lady, and Estelle Taylor, wife of Jack Dempsey,
in the role of Lucretia Borgia.

Preceding the movie there was a demonstration of what
the Vitaphone can do in presenting concert numbers by famous
artists; the audience sees the performer in a close-up view
with the advantage that those in the rear of the theater get
a clearer impression than if the performer were there in
life; the music created reaches the audience sometimes as
vivid as if it were the real thing.

Will H. Hays, director general of organized motion pictures, made a speech, via motion picture and Vitaphone, in which he said, "The future of motion pictures is as far-flung as all the to-morrows." He congratulated those who have produced the synchronization of picture and sound, and indicated that the movies of the future are to be bound up with mechanical devices for bringing music to as widespread audiences as those of the motion picture world.

During the reeling of the photoplay, Don Juan, the audience heard a running accompaniment by the New York Philharmonic Orchestra. The illusion of an actual orchestra creating the music was often complete.

The character of Don Juan is a dual role for Barrymore. First he is a Spanish grandee tricked by his wife; he kills her lover by a device known to readers of Balzac; he tells his son to believe in no woman. The son, played by Barrymore, is a philanderer of proportions and excess; the tale moves through many dark affairs with Rome for a background and the time of the Borgias as the period.

A house filled with representative first-nighters from the triple fields of motion pictures, music and drama, greeted the performance. Also there was a sprinkling of those highly developed persons who are interested in the new discoveries and inventions of that two-legged creature, man; they came representing civilization with hoping eyes on the future.

Sept. 16, 1926

Variety

And now in our midst we have Variety, the long-awaited Variety, the much-praised Variety.

The electric sign talents of Balaban and Katz are spelling the name Variety in dusky red lights in front of the Roosevelt Theater.

For an original photoplay there should be an original electric sign.

We are pleased to say that Variety has come into our

midst, that it was worth waiting for and at last seeing, that it has not been praised too much.

Emil Jannings, the male star, does the best all-around work we have seen from his prolific and changeful face, while Lya De Putti*, the new female star, is far out of the ordinary and will be discussed freely among ten or twenty million moviegoers in this country during the coming year.

The story is one of the oldest known in the annals of the human family; a man leaves one woman for another and the second woman double-crosses him for a handsomer man; there is murder and retribution.

And the old story is handled skillfully, is made the string on which many lanterns of themes, exploits and expressions are set forth in shadows, glimmer and blaze.

The characters are show people, and the atmosphere is that of the show world; we see marvelous vaudeville and superb trapeze feats.

In making the picture they realized there was vast opportunity for play of light, for contrasts and looming shadowgraphs in the realms of trapeze performance where there are double and triple somersaults, and an actor swings blindfolded in midair.

Variety is one of the few sure masterpieces of film art. Those who want novelty, a change from the usual, may find it here; those who want storytelling, character, atmosphere, along with a wizardry of photography, direction and stage management, will make no mistake about seeing Variety.

Sept. 14, 1926

That remarkable photoplay Variety is in its closing three days; it is to be shown in a limited run at neighborhood theaters; its run of two weeks at the Roosevelt Theater is a short one; that the crowds have not been larger may

---

*Variety, produced in Germany, made De Putti, a former belly dancer from Hungary, a star in America, but she died in 1931 at age 30.

indicate one thing or another; we leave the psychologists who think they know public taste to figure it out.

Variety is a masterly piece of film drama from several points of view, whether of story, of characters, of general atmosphere, of photographic art, sets, lighting, or of direction.

This reviewer has seen Variety three times, and will slip into the Roosevelt for one more view, if occasion offers. It is a varied box of tricks, a swift and shifting lot, of facts and illusions with which this picture deals. The events as told, and the characters as developed, have a little of the mystery of life itself; the disclosure is by a high order of art, intelligence and technical skill.

Understand--Variety isn't what some people might call a highbrow picture. Not by a long shot. It would interest any child interested in circuses, trapeze acting with triple somersaults, acrobats and juggling--and then besides its gaiety it tells a story at moments wayward and brutal but no more so than some of the books of Charles Dickens, for instance.

We have heard several persons who saw The Music last winter, and who have been to see Variety, make their declarations that as a work of art they would give Variety a higher rating. Of course, their opinions are personal.

Oct. 1, 1926

Variety, the European masterpiece of film drama, which has brought much comment that more productions of this type should be brought to this country and put on exhibition as pacemakers to some of our American directors, is the feature at the Castle Theater this week.

One important player in the cast of this picture is the Berlin Wintergarten audience that watches the trapeze act. The faces of rows of spectators are shown, the eyes and nostrils of individual onlookers captured, in curiosity, expectation as to what is happening or what turn of luck might happen high in the dome of the building where the performers are executing double and triple somersaults.

The motion picture can do this thing, and does it regularly, in a way that the legitimate drama cannot. Audiences as part of stage drama must be limited to the size of the stage. But in a motion picture play an audience may be enormous, and the circling, panoramic camera gathers it all and passes it to the projection machine, which throws it on the little screen, where the little human eye gathers it as if it were reality.

The crowd may be in the Wintergarten in Berlin, it may be at a big league or World Series ball game, it may be in the Yale Bowl seeing football or at the Hollywood Bowl in song service or at pontifical mass of the Eucharist Congress, in the stadium of Soldiers' Field. We have seen all these crowds employed with dramatic effect on the screen.

In Variety there is an exceptional skill in the portrayal of the crowd of spectators of the trapeze act.

Oct. 11, 1926

Greta Garbo as The Temptress

It is not the way of Greta Garbo to eat rose leaves in order to show filmgoers that she is an idle, destructive female. Vampires used always to do this. Some of them yet register wantonness by consuming a big bowl of deep red roses while they roll their eyes at some "helpless" he-man who is being sent simply off his nut by the sight of so much beauty.

Greta Garbo tempts in her own way, very cool of manner, very easy, and very, very sure. Where Lya De Putti is all fire and flesh, Greta Garbo is half-myth, the spirit of unmoral, not immoral, love, wavering and trailing through the picture, The Temptress, like the essence of all siren hearts over time.

In The Temptress she may be seen to take a nominal husband to protect her vampiring raids among the fatuous bankers of Paris; also she may be seen to lead one banker to dramatic and howling suicide. And, moreover, for six whole reels she sets an engineering camp in the Argentine so mad with desire that a mammoth dam is destroyed by jealous rivals, friends saber each other to death and two men duel viciously with wicked blacksnake whips.

For all the deaths she occasions, reputations she wrecks and life-works she ruins, this heroine of Blasco Ibañez somehow is urged upon you as "blameless, as sinned against rather than sinning," as the traditional female whose mere beauty causes sin to flourish.

Greta Garbo, slim, pale, like willows turning yellow in autumn, is the one actress, sure enough, to put into this role if it is to be made plausible. Gowned to kill, directed in such a manner that her face is full into the camera most of the time, she scores a downright triumph.

Antonio Moreno, Roy D'Arcy, Lionel Barrymore, Marc MacDermott, Robert Adamson--all good people for their roles-- have a lot to do in this long special from Metro-Goldwyn-Mayer's workshops. Fred Niblo, who made Ben Hur, worked on this and shows again his talents for arresting, vivid scenes and his inabilities to humanize plot.

Presentation is at the Roosevelt, where Greta Garbo may be recommended as something indeed for all adults to look upon.

Nov. 24, 1926

What Price Glory

One moment--you're in the busy whirl of traffic in Randolph Street--the next you're away off in France living again the war as vividly, as dramatically, as real as you'll ever be able to live it eight years or a hundred years after it's over.

That's the Aladdin transformation which awaits one who goes into the Garrick to see the screen version of What Price Glory. William Fox, with Raoul Walsh directing and the help of a lot of men who have had a friendly speaking acquaintance with the late party over there, have taken this graphic tale of the great conflict and turned out a masterpiece that's hard to tell from the original.

It is the story of the comedy, the drama, the tragedy,
the harshness, the cruelty and the futility of the war as it
was lived by the men--and the women--who fought it.   It
isn't overplayed and it isn't theatrical.   It is the war in
stark reality--except, perhaps in that melodramatic ending,
which, let's hope, they put in more as a theoretical "kick"
rather than to be swallowed as an actuality.

Strangely enough, comedy forms the greater part of
this masterful yarn of the war, rich, uproarish, screaming
comedy.   But the drama and the tragedy is there, drama
that thrills and tragedy that grips.   The battle scenes, of
which there are many, tell the grim story of war as no
tongue or pen will ever tell it.   They are some of the great-
est at which a camera has ever clicked, either in the real or
make-believe.   The "big push, " the streaming over, the top,
the confusion, the terror, the spitting machine guns, the
roaring, tearing, thunderous barrages, are enough to make
any ex-participant want to dive for the nearest shell hole.

The story, of course, revolves around those two hard-
boiled, swearin' leathernecks, Capt. Flagg and Sergt. Quirt,
and their eternal clash over the feminine spoils of war.
Victor McLaglen is the battered-nosed, foul-mouthed, hard-
ened captain and Edmund Lowe is the tough sergeant.   They
are everthing Laurence Stallings and Maxwell Anderson must
have had in mind when they wrote the story.   Dolores Del
Rio is the charming, chic, delectable Charmaine who reminds
you so much of the girl you left behind--over there.

The cussin' in the stage play that shocked pious souls
is there, too.   Not in subtitles, but it's there--if, like the
preacher's son, you know all the words and can read lip
movements.

Maybe you missed the big show and wished you hadn't.
Maybe you didn't miss it and wished you had.   Either way
you'll be sorry if you miss What Price Glory.   It's war as
real as you'll ever see it, and withal it's a sermon on
peace, for in it you'll find, as nearly as you'll ever find,
the answer to that question--what price glory, anyway?

Nov. 27, 1926

The Movies Are

At regular intervals we meet the intelligent and culti-
vated person of refinement who feels that the movies are not
entitled to much observation or consideration from those who
are looking forward toward a higher human uplift.

Usually, we find that such persons consider Black
Beauty quite a horse, and the book about Black Beauty should
be in the list of every young child's reading. Or they be-
lieve that Bob, Son of Battle or Buck, the dog of Jack London's
Call of the Wild are important dogs for young people to know
about.

Yet such is the swiftness of our motion picture civiliza-
tion, and so wide the extent of the photoplay area of display,
that it is easily safe to say that there are hundreds, thousands
of children, as well as young and old people, who are familiar
with certain horses and dogs of the films, but have never
heard of these other animals.

A hundred thousand are familiar with Tony, the Tom
Mix horse, for a thousand who know Black Beauty.

A hundred thousand and more are close acquaintances
with Rin-Tin-Tin as compared with the thousand or less who
know Buck or White Fang or Bob, Son of Battle.

And the movie fans know these animals in a way that
readers of books of fiction seldom know their animals.

Black Beauty, for instance, is a sort of animal cracker
animal; it is taken as handed on; it does not smite its be-
holders with the living glow and shine of Tom Mix's Tony,
pawing his hoofs and impatiently waiting for his master or
arching his glossy neck as the master pets him after a fast
ride dripping with sweat and defeating the enemies of justice.

We recall two men in argument once about Shakespeare,
one of them summarizing it with "Shakespeare is."

The movies are.

Men and women of culture may be aloof, as they please,
or they may try to look at them patronizingly, with no eye
for the motives of producers and no ear for the points urged
by Elder Will Hays.

The cold, real, upstanding fact holds--the movies are.
They come so close to pre-empting some functions hitherto
held exclusively by the school and university systems that the
philosopher of civilization who doesn't take them into con-
sideration with broad, sympathetic measurement is in danger
of being in the place of the drum major of the band who
marched up a side street while the band went straight along
on the main stem--without leadership.

Dec. 18, 1926

Although the silent film industry was about to perish,
the silent film itself was reaching its apex. In a similar
paradox, Sandburg was still growing as a reviewer as his
other literary efforts were propelling him beyond the status
of a mere chronicler of the cinema. Already, as his repu-
tation grew, he transcended the role of motion picture editor.
In March, he won a new two-column logo ("From the Note-
book of Carl Sandburg") with his picture, and as often as
not, he wrote of Midwest folklore and miscellany rather than
movies. Not that there weren't good movies to review.
Metropolis, Underworld (written by his Daily News colleague
Ben Hecht), Wings, Flesh and the Devil, It, and of course,
The Jazz Singer caught his attention. The first film with
synchronized dialogue and music, The Jazz Singer, even more
than the previous year's Don Juan, seized the public's atten-
tion about the possibilities of sound.

The Sheer Magic of What Price Glory

Here is a strange matter. Here is a motion picture
with homely ruffians for heroes, with a faithless flirt for a
heroine, with an unorthodox ending and with blasphemy and
profanity and suggestion coursing through it--here is a pic-
ture rich with all the taboos, achieving the unquestioned tri-
umph of the season.

What Price Glory violates every maxim in the screen
director's guidebook and literally bowls over the very people
for whom these guidebooks were prepared.

Housewives, grandmothers, orthodox matrons in hun-

dreds sit thrilling and weeping and shaking with laughter most
strangely and inexplicably in the Garrick Theater these days.
They have never done anything but flee from such factors in
real life.   They have never loved drunken, carnal screen
characters before.   Probably they never will again.   But they
do these days in the Garrick.

The thing is sheer magic.   Sheer necromancy in its
heroizing of two battered, foul-tongued professional soldiers.
Capt. Flagg and Sergt. Quirt come to the screen as stronger,
better-rounded characters than to the stage.   Lawrence Stal-
lings and Maxwell Anderson made them famous.   Raoul Walsh
and William Fox made them immortal.   It is the camera that
must receive the credit.   It is the camera that erects, in
its shots of Flagg's head, such a statue to the ancient pro-
fessional soldier as Phidias could never have done.

Here is the secret for the incredible popular triumph
of What Price Glory on the screen.   It rises above the ap-
peals of patriotism, sentiment, humor, and romance--although
it has all those things--to shake the whole emotional structure
of spectators with an epic portrait of two fascinating and vio-
lent men.   It rises to the heights of doing the professional
soldier as he has waited 5,000 years to be done, without
gloves, without patronage and with sure, certain truthfulness.

The professional soldier swears, he wastes his leisure
on scarlet women, he drinks, he carouses, he is vulgar and
brutal.

Well, he was so in the camps of Caesar, Alexander,
Napoleon and Frederick the Great.

The hard-boiled fighting man violates every canon of
the respectable civilian.   Well, it was so in the legions of
Gustavus Adolphus, of Cyrus the Great and William Tecumseh
Sherman.

The man who fights as a trade, rather than for any
flag or slippered burgher, has his kindly moments, his codes
of honor, his manliness in odd moments in battle lulls.

This was true in the ranks of Hannibal and Marshall
Ney.

What Price Glory soars above all rules and canons of
picture-making because it holds to these truths.   The broken-
nosed head of Flagg as it comes through the smoke, cool,

bitter, deadly, while young marines drop, drop, drop behind him and Germans shoot, run and fall before him, is the head of Caesar.

The face Flagg turns to the light-of-love Charmaine as he comes out of the trenches on leave is the face all professional warriors have turned to the crimson vivandiere since war was war.

Becoming the tale of two age-old characters, romance, adventure, humor all become merely obbligatos to a saga, a hero-song.

From the moment What Price Glory begins until it ends it can do nothing, say nothing that is not in the epic mold. Victor McLaglen may be a good actor but he is something finer than that here. He is Capt. Flagg; he is Caesar. Edmund Lowe may be close to him in artistry but he is almost as completely Sergt. Quirt, Alexander the Great kissing Persian camp-followers after the day's red work is done. Dolores del Rio suddenly seems to be a great actress. She is nothing of the kind. She is merely the perfect sweetheart of those laughing, faithless men who seldom marry because they are too busy defending whole populations of women whom they never see, nor care to see.

Jan. 15, 1927

Films' Effect on Farm Boys

There is always much curiosity about just what Will Hays does in his adjusting of the movies to the best interests of the public. Now and then one hears of his having refused to let movie-makers film such a salacious novel. Again come rumors of his having made careless picture personalities mend their ways.

From his office in New York comes, among other items which chronicle the uses of motion pictures, an interview with an educator who annually watches over some 5,000 students. This educator, President Harold C. Lewis of the Coyne Electrical School, which gives technical schooling to youths of moderate means, tells of the moral fortifications movies have given farm boys for their assault upon the city.

"From interviewing approximately 2,500 farm or farm-town boys each year," says the educator, "I note, in the last decade, a disappearance of the 'greenhorn.' Country boys of to-day aren't the innocent dupes and prey of metropolitan adventuresses as were their fathers. To-day they are able to take care of themselves, to sidestep the temptations of the great city as are city-bred boys.

"The reason for this progress lies mainly in motion pictures. For over a decade the movies have been frequently displaying the manners and customs of so-called 'gold-diggers, temptresses, etc. The excitement of society, or gayety of night life in big cities, has been a popular theme with motion pictures and as a result the rustic youth arriving in town to-day is not bowled over or fooled by seemingly brilliant sophistication. Movies have taught him to dress, to eat, to conduct himself with about as much self-possession as city youths.

"Parents in rural America may worry about their young-sters attending the movies too much, but they can worry less than they did about the youngsters when they go the the city."

Jan. 22, 1927

Only W.C. Fields

When Pa Potter, goat of his family and butt of high-pressure stock salesmen, suddenly finds that the oil shares he has foolishly purchased are worth a fortune, he puts on one of the funniest three minutes that the screen has ever carried.

He does it as only W.C. Fields can do this sort of thing. Fields, the screen's leading expert at doing fumbling, foolish characters, celebrates Pa Potter's one big moment in a drab career by tearing the dull, prim livingroom to shreds; he whoops, he bounds, he kicks pillows, he tosses 200 pieces of sheet music into the air and bucks around the little apart-ment like nothing so much as a Clydesdale mare with a horsefly fast to the middle of its back.

In corners his family cowers. Fields is free; he is doing the sort of thing he does best, light-headed, trivial-minded chaos. And he does it so that no one will ever dare do it again.

W. C. Fields plays J. P. McEvoy's <u>The Potters</u> for all he is worth, which is considerable, and for all it is worth, which is somewhat less. The slight story, by rights, should be told in a two-reel comedy, but thanks to the genius of Fields it fills out seven spools with a high average of laughter.

In Fields' hands, <u>Pa Potter</u> becomes far more of a character than in either McEvoy's humorous articles or stage comedy. Fields makes him the blunderer supreme, the eternal butt and goat with figments of cuteness coming and going in his stupid head, and with just enough humanity and realism in his art to keep Potter safe in your affections. Fields' supporting cast here is inconsequential. Paramount made it and the Oriental Theater displays it as a companion attraction to Paul Ash.

Jan. 28, 1927

Fields--A Great Comedian

W. C. Fields, even without the tennis balls he used to juggle in <u>The Follies</u>, is a great comedian. Nobody better than he, not even Chaplin, knows the gestures, the alert movements, the quick jumps that light the fuse of laughter and nobody can be more abject and pitiful that he in his moments of dejection. The fact that he is getting on, that he is a man of experience, that he has, in Huxley's words, "warmed both hands at the fire of life," gives him a mellowness that the younger screen comedians lack. It is not slapstick humor that makes W. C. Fields amusing, it is fidelity to human nature at its weakest and funniest.

In <u>Running Wild,</u> the picture which divides time with Paul Ash's show at the Oriental this week, Fields plays the part of a poor worm which eventually turns.

Elmer Finch is the second husband of a shrewish wife and stepfather to her spoiled son. Finch has a daughter of his own, who tries to help him be a man, but finds the job almost beyond her. So much for his position at home. In business it is much the same. He has worked twenty years as bookkeeper without ever having had an increase in pay and nothing in his work has ever warranted his employer giving him one. He does, however, make an effort to increase his usefulness, but with disastrous results to himself and to the firm.

Finally he falls into the hands of a professional hypnotist who gives him a courage he had hitherto woefully lacked. He then sets out to do all the things he had wanted to do, but had not known how to accomplish. His "furore transitoria," as the brain specialists have it, lasts long enough for him to subdue all who have opposed him and in the end he is respected and happy, and the pretty much put-upon daughter comes into her own happiness when the young man of her choice wins her father over.

Mary Brian is the girl, Claude Buchanan the young man. Marie Shotwell plays an ungrateful part in the disagreeable stepmother, and Barney Raskie, as Junior, is the meanest, hatefulest cub of a boy that one could imagine. The cast is not a long one, but it is well chosen.

Running Wild is not an epoch-making picture, but it does give the star an opportunity for excellent character work.

July 14, 1927

It

Someone pretty sensible handled It.

Always, before, Elinor Glyn's* stories made producers, directors, continuity writers howl and bellow when filming time came. It used to be a hard job to make her characters human and genuinely romantic when filmed.

But when they came to film It, which madame had written to expound her new theory of what attracts people of opposing sexes, they tossed madame's story to the cruel waves that roar on the Pacific rocks. They kept the name It and

---

* Glyn (1864-1943) was a novelist best known for a supposedly erotic scene in her 1907 romance Three Weeks involving a tiger skin rug. The passage prompted an anonymous poetaster to write: "Would you like to sin/ With Elinor Glyn/ On a tiger skin?/ No, I'd prefer/ To err/ With her/ On some other fur."

made Mme. Glyn feel good by leading her on like a queen to
be photographed as herself explaining what It is to Antonio
Moreno.

But the story which runs in a current magazine is not
at all like the film, not like it in any respect, not even the
names of the characters.

The screen It is smart, funny and real.   It makes a
full-size star of Clara Bow and it hits William Austin out of
the minor class into the upper crust of screen comedians.

Miss Bow is a warm-hearted, smart alec, bewitching
little shop girl.   She stands behind the lingerie counter look-
ing impudently and longingly at the handsome owner of the
great department store.   As she does so her employer's
"silly-ass" friend, Mr. Austin, comes through the store
looking for people with "It." He had read Elinor Glyn's
declaration that some people have "It" and some do not; that
"It" is a strange quality that you recognize immediately.
Luckily, Mr. Austin looks at Clara Bow and calls out "She
has 'It.'"

He is right.

The plot is Clara's conquest of her employer.   The
interest of the picture is the bright stimulation of looking at
Clara, of laughing at the subtitles, which are funny, and
looking at Clara again.   She's most likely another Swanson.

Feb. 11, 1927

The Winning Clara Bow

Clara Bow seems to be winning in the race of flappers.

Every time the flapper-fillies go by Clara's eyes seem
to be more noticeably ahead of her rivals.   Her hair gets
wilder and wilder in the breeze and she loses more and more
harness.

In Rough-House Rosie she is down to running togs and
she goes like lightning.   Her role of Rosie demands that
she dress like a prizefighter, don white kid boxing gloves

and sock her little chorus-girl playmates right and left inside
the satin ropes of a night club. In such a costume and role
Clara is herself. She can romp more irresistibly, flirt more
convincingly and tease more impishly than any other of those
film girls who practice these arts, and Rough-House Rosie
gives her full play.

Rosie is rough. A fresh youth kisses her as they race
through a tunnel on a Coney Island roller coaster and when
they emerge into the light of day the young man's hat is a
collar and both his eyes are black. An earnest and moral
young prizefighter grows weary of her flirtations and takes
a caveman kiss. He, too, goes down before Clara's right
swing.

But when Douglas Gilmore, very much the he-peacock,
takes Rosie to a party of "swells" and introduces her to the
cocktails and kisses that other men's wives and other women's
husbands are exchanging, the little tough girl marches out and
goes back to her prizefighter beau. The gashouse is royal
raiment when worn for virtue's sake.

All that there is to the picture is Clara. And Clara
seems enough to the Chicago Theater's patrons this week.

May 27, 1927

Faust

Faust, now finishing its engagement at the Randolph,
is one of the most beautiful of all works of the moving pic-
ture. It should be in the library of every art school and
museum of America. Before the artistic composition which
dominates every single scene, the players and the plot be-
come insignificant. Even Emil Jannings cannot steal this
picture from the art director. For once this vivid personal-
ity of the screen is shadowed, snowed under by the cameraman.

In the first reels it seems that he may "run off" with
the honors as he has done in every photoplay he touched.
At the Faust opening Jannings is the squat, toad-like Satan
of primitive Teutonic mythology, a soiled and awful creature,
something finely imagined and electrically conceived in Jan-
nings' sensitive brain. Here he is one with the eerie and

mystic scenic effects which Murnau*, the director, has con-
ceived. He belongs to the wild moors, the dead trees that
gesture madly against the bare night sky, the infernal rings
of fire that squirm at Satan's victims.

So long as Jannings sticks to his conception of Satan as
a fat and squalid old man with a reptile's mind, he is the
Jannings of Passion, The Last Laugh and Variety. But when
Mephistopheles, in the adaption of the Goethe version, casts
the rejuvenated Faust into fleshly romance, Jannings adopts
the conventional costume of grand opera tradition. He tries
to make himself wickedly handsome. Black silk, a rapier,
and lip stick adorn him--and all at once he is nothing but a
grand opera basso, artificial, skilled but spiritless.

Into the highly impressionistic, profoundly beautiful set-
tings Gosta Ekman and Camilla Horn as Faust and Marguerite
fit like Grecian god-statues into the Parthenon. Indeed, for
all the strenuous action of the story, Ekman as the youthful
Faust and Miss Horn as the melting Gretchen never lost that
peculiar sculptural perfection which the German picture mak-
ers first displayed in certain shots of Variety's characters.

Any good Hollywood cast would have done better by the
story, but no one in America would have dared so absolute
and uncompromising a piece of devotion to scenic beauty. No
one in Hollywood has yet freed his imagination to attempt the
toilsome, idealistic search for perfection that is shown in
Faust backgrounds, brackens at midnight, trees that Hokasai
would weep over, strange and terrible birds of hell flailing
the sky with their wings, and gardens filled with the very
ache of springtime.

Feb. 17, 1927

Flesh and the Devil

If there was ever, in screendom, as earnest an exchange
of kisses as that between John Gilbert and Greta Garbo in
Flesh and the Devil let him who knows of it speak now or
forever hold his peace. John and Greta play the love-making

---

*Friedrick Wilhelm Murnau (1889-1931) who had made
Nosferatu in 1922 before leaving Germany for Hollywood as
so many were doing at the time.

roles of this Sudermann drama with a sincerity and realism
that saves it from being pure sensationalism.

So high-keyed is this story, so rapturous and never-
ending are the embraces of its hero and heroine that it might
readily have toppled, in the filming, into mawkish sentimen-
talism.

But John and Greta, under the fine, sane direction of
Clarence Brown, make the lovers so real that Flesh and the
Devil becomes a screen triumph. In its showing at McVicker's
so far there has not been uttered from the audience a single
one of those satirical "smacks" with which embarrassed ado-
lescents are fond of greeting lengthy kissing on the screen.

Fervent Flesh and the Devil is, but never unhuman, nor
over romantic.

Sudermann* told a tale of extravagant emotions, of a girl
unable to be true and of the two boyhood friends whom she
came between.   One of these youths is Gilbert and one is
Lars Hanson.   The one played by Gilbert is cajoled and cap-
tivated by this enigmatic, ardent girl and entangled in her
wiles before he discovers her husband. A duel. The. hus-
band dies. The lovers are to marry after a decent interval.
The army sends him away for a year and when he returns
he finds the girl wedded to his bosom friend. Even that is
not enough to kill love in him, and when the girl, helpless
before her own wantonness, is eager to elope with him, he
agrees in sobbing torment.   The denouement is unexpected,
but inescapable and of a superior sort of happiness.

Miss Garbo is hereafter a star to be reckoned with, so
perfectly does she create a character for the heroine, lovely,
pitiful, thrilling Felicitas, who drifts downward without ever
realizing that the world holds such things as morals.

                                                    Feb. 18, 1927

                        The Scarlet Letter

Lillian Gish has been in a good many terrible fixes in

---

*Hermann Sudermann, of Germany (1857-1928), in his
novel The Undying Past.

her screen career, but none more pitiable than when, in The
Scarlet Letter, she is manacled down to the stocks on Boston
Commons and made a shameful object lesson to the young
Puritans for having skipped and run on the Sabbath.

Those little white hands of Lillian's hang in resignation,
her mock face, minus hate, droops and there she sits, under
the placard of shame, waiting for the Puritan fathers to come
clumping back to lift her sentence.

All Hester Prynne had done, up to that time, had been
to chase her canary through the woods on Sunday morning
and, in the course of the pursuit, to have skipped once and
patted her hands together twice. Such an infernal display of
happiness and joy outraged the Puritans on their way to church
and they had Hester thrown into the stocks.

The Puritans catch thunder all through Victor Seastrom's
film version of Hawthorne's novel, The Scarlet Letter. They
are depicted as fanatical, cruel, pathological in their love of
inflicting pain. They sew a scarlet letter "A" on Hester's
bosom to brand her with shame for not having told what man
was the father of her child. They spy on merrymakers,
listen for gossip, snoop up and down the aisles of churches
thumping on the head men who fall asleep. They fuss with
little children about their beliefs and souls and devils. They
enjoy persecuting and being persecuted.

And when they summon poor, delicate, beautiful Lillian
Gish up to the pillory to be branded with "the scarlet letter"
you will wish for nothing so much as a horde of red Indians
to be coming over the stockades and through the town, mas-
sacring the Puritan fathers, even at the sacrifice of Thanks-
giving dinners.

The Scarlet Letter is a Hawthorne classic, filmed in
the honesty to the spirit of the story and with sufficient close-
ness to the letter to escape the censors. To it Lillian Gish
gives one of her unrivaled performances, spiritual and human
both, exaltedly imaginative and artistic.

But the picture is more than a starring vehicle for
Miss Gish. It is quite a show on its own hook, big, mag-
nificently historical, powerfully dramatic. Hawthorne wrote
a daring story. Seastrom turned it into a picture that dares
to be poignant and poetic in the midst of sensational happen-
ings such as branding, desertions, seductions, public con-
fessions of sin and moral accusations.

Its local debut is at the Chicago Theater this week.

Mar. 21, 1927

The Griffith Style

D.W. Griffith remains the creative artist.

Born in Kentucky, where the talk every evening in the lamplight was of pioneers, he is still the pioneer of motion pictures, still exploring new horizons, opening up new fields, hacking ahead, traveling alone in spirit, at least.

Like Daniel Boone, who won the Dark and Bloody Ground, but who neglected to file it under his own name, Griffith had neglected to put a fortune aside for himself. Pioneers have frequently been of such admirable folly. Nowadays Griffith works for the big producers who came along after his first pioneerings and filed on the land he cleared. This confuses him a little. But it does not keep him from striking out after new ideas now and then.

He hits on what may be developed into a new screen technic in parts of his Sorrows of Satan, now at McVicker's The melting of shadows into other shadows, the criss-crossing of shadows to converge eventually into the sardonic, polished face of Adolphe Menjou, a mocking and modern Satan, is as interesting coinage of Griffith's mind as was the "close-up," the "mist portraits" and a dozen other inventions of his in other days. Also the myth scenes which introduce Sorrows of Satan, those eerie moments when Jehovah's angels, under Michael, cast forth from paradise the rebellious hordes of Satan, are Griffith at his most inventive and dramatic best.

Sorrows of Satan has the sense of vastness, chaos, originality, and sudden interludes of unimagined beauty that make Griffith so much akin, in his present stage, to Walt Whitman, the poet. There was a time when Griffith was a Charles Dickens and Walt Whitman in one. Lately the Whitman predominates. He no longer tells stories as directly and absorbingly as once he did.

Marie Corelli was no author for Griffith to attempt to

follow in screening. Her novel, <u>Sorrows of Satan</u>, is flimsy, sensational, hectic. In trying to justify it for his own use Griffith evidently suffered, for the story his picture tells is neither Corelli nor Griffith.

Still, everything Griffith does is worth anyone's time. <u>Sorrows of Satan</u> is not enough to enhance Griffith's reputation, but it would make his reputation if he had been heretofore unknown. The old magic of his touch burns in scenes wherein two starving writers, a boy and a girl, blend their sufferings and ideas, in frigid garrets. It lives again in the orgies of London bohemias where Satan, in evening clothes, takes the boy to wean him from his love and his ideas. The picture is rich in emotion, in gripping episodes, in momentary moods, which will absorb any onlooker who does not have the misfortune to be always looking, through filmdom, for another <u>Broken Blossoms</u> or <u>Intolerance</u>.

The cast is competent. Menjou, Ricardo Cortez, Carol Dempster and Lya de Putti have the star roles.

Mar. 23, 1927

A Critic Is...

We have on our desk a publication put out once a month by one of the biggest motion-picture corporations. We notice that John Grierson*, an independent critic, has this to say: " 'The Wanderer' had a great story (the parable of the Prodigal Son), but the telling made it less than great. 'The Sea Beast' had a magnificent story (the greatest story in American literature, 'Moby Dick') but the telling made it nothing at all. On the other hand, 'Variety' had a very unoriginal story but the telling made it one of the great successes on Broadway. 'The Merry Widow' was a musical comedy trifle to begin with, but the telling made it one of the more powerful things of the year. 'Beau Geste' was a simple mystery story, but the telling made it jump for a while into epic. 'The Vanishing American' was a Zane Grey western, but the telling made it for a couple of reels great

*The British doucmentary maker (1898-1972) who founded the National Film Board of Canada.

history. 'The Last Laugh' was the simple story of an old
man who was deprived of a uniform, but the telling made it
the tragic little bijou of the highbrows."

We consider this marvelous movie criticism. We praise
the critic. He thinks just what we think, and writes exactly
as we have written about all of these photoplays. The good
critic, the dandy critic, is the one whose mind runs with our
mind and whose personal taste is like our own.

Mar. 3, 1927

Babe Comes Home

Some fifty or sixty times a year the portly party whom
small boys know as "the sultan of swat" or "the pachyderm of
punch" or something like that takes his bat and knocks base-
balls into the laps of people a great distance from him. For
that he is famous, so famous that it now seems likely small
boys of 2027 A.D. will still talk of him. For that, too, he
has been paid amazingly not only by his baseball employers,
but by the motion picture people who have filmed his person-
ality in a baseball drama, Babe Comes Home.

This motion picturization of Babe Ruth holds forth now
at the Roosevelt, where the whoops of excited males can be
heard exactly as at the Sox park the other day when Babe in
the flesh was playing.

Babe Comes Home is lean on story and fat on Ruth.
The drama is not so long as a bat or so deep as a piece of
baseball strategy, but it's enough--it serves. It shows Ruth
hitting, running and sliding. It gives remarkable closeups
of the "Bambino" at his work. And it reveals interesting
reasons for the really colossal popularity of George Herman
Ruth. For one thing it shows him to be frolicsome, amiable
and winning in his personality. He photographs surprisingly
well and whatever in the way of comedy his director has
asked him to do, he has done with whole-hearted gusto. There
is genuine humor in his face when, to help a frightened girl,
he plunges under a bed after a mouse and emerges with a
mousetrap clamped on his finger.

Like "Red" Grange, this other athletic marvel is sur-

prisingly good as an actor.   Perhaps the control of muscle
and nerve they have learned in sport makes them unusually
responsive in obeying film direction.

Anyway the great "Babe" is here in closeups aided and
abetted by so trained a "trouper" as Anna Q. Nilsson, whose
pleas it is, in the ninth inning, that inspire the despondent
player to whack the ball far, far away into the lap of the un-
known bleacherite who always catches Ruth's home runs.

                                                        May 13, 1927

                              Canine Capers

Rin-Tin-Tin, the dog being starred in films with such
success by Warner Brothers,   demonstrates again his almost
human powers in Tracked by the Police, the picture at the
State-Lake.

As the protector and companion of the young hero in
charge of building a big irrigation dam in Arizona, he per-
forms feats that make one marvel at the dog's sagacity and
powers of reasoning.   He moves levers, turns cranks and
does whatever else is required around machinery to make
it perform and in all ways proves himself eligible for nom-
ination as an entry in the next auto race, so capable is he
of making engines behave.   He also opens barred and bolted
doors, climbs out of a deserted mine, carries messages
along a narrow elevation miles and miles in length, backs
up a stairway and over rafters, assumes a limp and dis-
criminates between friend and foe with unerring judgment.

Rin-Tin-Tin is called upon to do these things on behalf
of the company building the dam and opposed by a rival irri-
gation company which bribes the crew to delay the work and
when it can no longer stall, to attempt to wreck the whole
works.

Jason Robards, who is coming along well in pictures,
plays the young engineer in charge, and Tom Santschi, the
evil genius of the picture, is both evil and a genius for dev-
iltry.   Both are earnest and capable, and young Robards is
a manly hero.

Virginia Browne Faire is more than just a pretty girl in the picture. She has few scenes, but those she has are telling and require higher powers of acting than most movie roles. She plays the daughter of the man whose fortune has gone into the irrigation project, but who is laid low with an injury just when the work needs him most.

There is a feeling that the censors must have made some heavy cuts in the film. For instance, the finish of Santschi is indefinite and one does so want to see him "get his." It is pretty certain that he is swallowed up in the broiling torrent he has set loose, but that and some of the scenes between the villain and the girl end abruptly. Not for such as us, the movie censors must have thought.

Scenery is superb with beautiful canine figures silhouetted against the sky. There is much that is beautiful and much, too, that thrills and excites the sympathies.

June 2, 1927

Eddie Cantor Reborn

Eddie Cantor appears to have washed his face and graduated from black face comedy once and for all. He is the funmaker of the screen comedy, Special Delivery, on the program of youth and frolic this week at the Oriental and plays a rookie mail carrier, who keeps his eyes and ears open and proves himself not only a "great lover," but a first-rate secret service man.

The picture is a riot of fun. Cantor's big, solemn eyes, which belie his innate capacity for being amusing, have full play on the screen. His physical makeup and his jerky gestures win laughs for him even without the "gags" or funny stunts which have been so carefully thought out.

To make his girl jealous he appears in a balcony scene with a dressed-up dummy which is one of the signals for laughter. He does a dance on the floor at the mail carriers' ball, which is nothing but the squirming of an agile man with a piece of ice down his back, but it wins him the cup in the contest of the black bottom dance. He takes a ride with a motorcycle "cop," which makes the audience gasp by its perils, and he finally rushes to the docks to save the girl he loves from the clutches of the scheming villain.   He does this by commandeering the hook and ladder of the fire department and getting himself on the deck of the moving vessel by having the ladder deposit him on board.

The risks to life and limb are enormous, as is the fashion in the comedies of the experts, Harold Lloyd, Syd Chaplin and the others, and Special Delivery, in spite of the simplicity of its plot, has plenty of thrilling moments.

Jobyna Ralston, once chief foil and leading lady for Harold Lloyd, plays the girl for whom Cantor risks his neck in Special Delivery.   She is so well used to the work laid out for her that she does it simply, cleverly and courageously. Miss Ralston is pretty without being a great beauty and is a likable actress.

William Powell is the villain de luxe.   He delivers some hard blows on the reed-like anatomy of his adversary, but in the end he is delivered over to justice and walks out of the picture with a sneer on his handsome face which would do credit to the most gentlemanly crook.

The cast of principals is not a large one, but the supernumeraries are countless as they appear in the various scenes.

A word of praise is due the subtitles.   Their sparing use of words is notable.   "Take him," the hero says to the heroine as she tells of the offer she has had from her rich employer.   "Take him.   I am a failure.   Three years ago dad told me not to come home until I had made $3,000.   At present I owe $16," fingering the dress suit he has rented.

The throb of pity for the poor weakling is followed quickly by the ready laugh.   It is that kind of picture and Eddie Cantor is that kind of comedian.

June 17, 1927

Metropolis

The complaint of the motion picture theater men in the past has been that, while everybody praises German movies when they are shown on this continent, nobody goes to see them.

Americans whoop and carry on about what wonderful
pictures Passion, The Golem, Dr. Caligari, Variety and Faust
were and write big letters to the newspapers demanding to
know why the public doesn't get more pictures like those.
But when those pictures were running the American people
were not at all worried about showing the theater man that
he was a benefactor of art because he presented great pic-
tures.

It may be that Metropolis, now at the Roosevelt Theater,
will break this spell or hoodoo, whatever you want to call it.

Metropolis has a sensational idea understandable to any-
body and capable of being enjoyed by anyone who likes to
speculate on the future. It has scientists who, in a mammoth
laboratory, create a mechanical woman, utilizing electricity
in a way that is expected to be common in 2900 A.D. This
woman is beautiful, but without any morals or conscience.
For night clubs in this city of a thousand years from now
she does a skirtless dance that is contrary to all but Moslem
laws, and for the millions of workers in their depths she
preaches revolution, destruction, general hades. She is
beautiful, seductive, ruinous and is played with a serpentine,
pagan skill by Brigitte Helm, the alluring German actress.

Anyone who had a good time at The Lost World will
have a better time at Metropolis, for it carries the spectator
into the world of a thousand years hence. No such settings
have ever been attempted before on the screen, not even in
Intolerance. Buildings rise like mountains in the air. Thou-
sands of feet up are curving causeways for automobiles, others
for pedestrians, at other heights are airways for behemoth
airplanes. Down under the city in subterranean caverns are
the monstrous machines by which the city is operated. There,
too, are the workers, dumb, cattle-like hordes, who lockstep
with beaten spirit, thousands and thousands of them, to the
huge elevators which carry them in twelve-hour shifts to their
duties.

The entire city is controlled by one man, John Master-
man, financial overlord and industrial Napoleon. It is the
workings of the plot that bring him down at last when the
mechanical woman, the creature of his laboratories, spurs
his slaves to revolt and wrecks the mountainous machines
about his ears.

Metropolis is photographed by Karl Freund*, who did
Variety and, for its photography alone, should not be missed.
It is easily the most interesting thing in our theaters today.

July 18, 1927

The Big Parade

On a second view of The Big Parade one has time to
think. No such opportunity is ever given anyone during a
first look at this achievement in emotionalism. Certainly
not since The Birth of a Nation has a picture so stormed the
emotions of its spectators. One must laugh, weep or fall into
love or hate with these characters which Stallings put on pa-
per and King Vidor transferred to the screen.

However, on a second visit there comes a chance to
consider things. For instance, those machine guns of the
enemy, which mow down the doughboys as they march through
the woods. Who has ever seen a human to equal them in
hatefulness? Slowly they climb to a pitch of villainy to which
no screen actor ever attained. It is not the men who point
the guns that we hate, it is the inanimate little rod that spits
death.

King Vidor shows it to you in flashes, cutting back to
the doughboys who are coming on, marching slowly, march-
ing steadily, with something of the inexorable rise of a thun-
derstorm--and with something, too, of the terrible solemnity
of death march music. They go down here, there in casual
topplings. Not one of them gesticulates heroically in the
mock agonies of actors. They simply drop and the death
walk goes on.

---

*Freund (1890-1969), a Czech, was an important figure in
the development of cinematography. A projectionist in Berlin
at 16, a newsreel cameraman at 18, he later opened a lab
and worked on many of F.W. Murnau's films. In 1929 he
came to Hollywood and in 1937 won an Oscar for his camera-
work on The Good Earth. In later years he found himself
working on television's I Love Lucy.

Will the machine guns reach the three doughboys about whom you care? It is a moment of aching suspense, and although it is a short scene, it seems hours long to spectators. Probably films never approached this suspense before or since; accomplished because it seems impossible that all three of the soldiers, John Gilbert, Karl Dane and Tom O' Brien, can, by any chance, escape the villain.

Vidor interrupts the suspence but once, and that when Karl Dane with great satisfaction and elaborate nonchalance shoots down from a tree the sniper who has been killing doughboys. Saintly old ladies, highly aesthetic customers, patrons of refinement now in McVickers, peal into laughter and delight as the gaunt Dane spurts derisive tobacco juice at his malicious foe.

But Vidor snatches the scene back into that terrifying suspense again a second later and the death walk goes on.

Many there are who insist that The Big Parade is the greatest of all pictures, but there are more who say, "Well, anyway, that march through the woods is the greatest scene motion pictures ever had."

July 25, 1927

Emil Jannings

They say that when Emil Jannings is working on a screen role his loving wife leaves him for the time, remaining away until such time as the picture is done and Emil his own amiable self again.

Night and day, the story goes, he lives his role, brooding, thinking, holding his mind to the limits of his dramatic character. He wears the kind of clothes the character would wear, talks like him, eats like him, thinks like him, goes to the studio in his costume ready for work.

The story seems plausible enough when Jannings' pictures reach town, for no artist, unless it be Charlie Chaplin, can achieve one-quarter of Jannings' reality in a role. No one ever came to the screen with such utter disappearance of self. To this day the movie-goers of the country have no definite and clear mental picture of what Jannings' own face looks like. It has changed so utterly from one picture to another as to make the man himself misty and far away. Which is only another way of saying that Jannings is incomparably the greatest of all screen actors, unless it be that the aforesaid Charles Spencer Chaplin can tie him.

The debut of Jannings in his first American picture does much to explode the theory that the Germans are greater than Americans in making pictures. This and that German director or cameraman has been hailed as a surpassing genius as the result of some German picture that reached America. But nine-tenths of those German masterpieces have had Emil Jannings as chief player and now that his first American picture, The Way of All Flesh, is seen to be another unquestionable masterpiece, it becomes evident that most of the genius of UFA's Berlin-made pictures has been nothing more or less than Jannings.

Any picture in which he plays looks superior, exceptional, packed with genius. His amazing ability to make audiences think and feel with him makes also directors, cameramen and other actors look superior. He lends naturalness to the whole picture, realism to every action.

In The Way of All Flesh, now at McVicker's, he is every bit as marvelous in depicting character and character-change, just as amazing in his capture of the minor bits of naturalism or of the thundering emotional climaxes, as he was in his series of German pictures from Passion to Variety.

His role is that of a Milwaukee banker, upstanding, domestic, good, who loses his name and reputation as the result of one fatal spree with the ruinous Phyllis Haver in a Chicago underworld honky-tonk.

As the aged derelict, Jannings achieves an aching intensity of sympathy, a poignancy such as the screen never saw before and which is almost too near to heartbreak to be withstood in any manner.

An incredibly good, mysteriously powerful performance.

Sept. 15, 1927

Wings

Nearly ten years after the end of the world war the
story of the war from the air is told in a stupendous picture
called Wings, which opened at the Erlanger last evening.

The ten years have brought some realistic stories of
the conflict, notably The Big Parade and What Price Glory,
not to mention the humorous Better 'Ole, but Wings, it would
seem, is bound to hold a place all its own and way above the
others in actual achievement, regardless of heart interest.

Because of the enormous difficulty of making the air
shots and the almost prohibitive cost, the air story of the
war has not been told until now. The picture was two years
in the making and taxed the resources of the Paramount stu-
dios. Even then it could not have been done without the co-
operation of the war department and the help of the navy planes.
Aces of the world war were called upon to assist and alto-
gether the production is something over which to marvel. It
is announced as a Lucien Hubbard production directed by
William A. Wellman.

Full recognition of all the obstacles comes when one
sees the picture, and no other film which can be called to
mind is capable of giving quite the same number of thrills.
Partly is this so because of the romance, the mystery, the
glamour of flying. Here are a dozen Lindberghs, it seems,
all courageous, all skillful and all engaged in a serious duty.

The love story running through it is a dignified one--
just the kind that happened in every one of our neighborhoods.
Two young chaps going away to war, both of them in love
with the same girl and one of them loved by another girl,
and the stay-at-homes all sorrowing. The idealistic friend-
ship between the two men is preserved as faithfully here as
it was in Beau Geste, and the small part a sweet girl at
home plays in their lives is delicately traced. Jobyna Ral-
ston is this girl. To Clara Bow falls the role of an Ameri-
can girl in war service in France. Her vivacity is kept
within bounds and she is a relief from the somber scenes of
war. With all this, care is taken that the feminine element
is made negligible. It is man's work that is being pictured
and men are the heroes. Richard Arlen, a veteran of the
world war, having served with the Royal Flying Corps of

Canada, is one of the youthful leads and Charles Rogers* is
the other.   Richard Tucker is seen as the air commander,
and a glimpse is given of Gary Cooper as Cadet White. Henry
B. Walthall is an invalid father of one of the flyers and the
rest of the cast is made of well-known names.

Oct. 31, 1927

Underworld

The scene is yesterday at noon.   The doors of the Roose-
velt Theater swing open and crowds wander out.   A "spill"
has come--a "spill" being the departure of large groups of
customers at the end of the picture.

Those faces look exhausted, eyes turn up and down
State Street as in a daze.   Underworld has left them limp,
these Chicagoans who have come to see the gunmen and gang-
sters of their city brought at last to the screen.

Within the theater packed rows of faces are staring as
the picture starts again on its endlessly circling path of sav-
agery.   Faces have been rapt and nerves have dangled in sus-
pense here before, but never like this.   Good reason, Under-
world has more suspense than almost any picture ever made
before.   Films there have been more realistic--The Last
Laugh, for instance. Films there have been more achingly
poignant--Broken Blossoms for one. But no work for the screen
ever approached this for sheer excitement, for intensity.

Ben Hecht, the Chicago reporter and novelist, wrote it
as his maiden scenario.   Josef von Sternberg, all artist, di-
rected it.   The business office inserted sentiment here and
there in the work of these two exotic geniuses, Hecht and von
Sternberg, but the story is theirs, between them and to their
score goes one of the great ones in screen history.

Over and above them, however, towers a new American
actor, George Bancroft.   Bancroft, even more than his author
or his director, is microscopically honest with his job.   He
plays "Bull" Weed, master-terror of the underworld, with com-

---

*Better known as Buddy Rogers (b. 1904), husband of Mary
Pickford.

plete conviction. He is like Wallace Beery, only better; he
is, at times, even-up in power with the greatest of them all,
Emil Jannings.   Indeed, in the swift, irresistible rush of
Underworld's first two reels, Bancroft reaches out from the
screen to seize his spectators and make them his as com-
pletely as Jannings ever did.

"Bull" Weed is king of the Chicago jungle.   "Attila at
the gates of Rome, " a laughing king who rescues bums from
the gutter and when they ask him what they can do for him,
gasps "Nobody helps me.   I help other people, " and then
breaks into jaguar guffaws.   "Bull" is good to "Feathers, "
his "moll. " He sticks up a jewel shop on Michigan Avenue
to get a diamond necklace Feathers craves, privately deeming
the ornament vulgar, though he does.

Bull Weed stops little boys stealing apples, advises them
not to rob, gives them big bills and boots their little poste-
riors while he bellows in merriment.

But when Bull Weed must hang for having killed "Buck"
Mulligan in the latter's flower shop, then Bancroft rises to
tragic majesty.   How he accomplishes it without sacrificing
his roughness, his toughness, his winning smile, only he
can tell.   But he does it.   Jail breaks, smashing machine-
gun battles with the police, vicious thumbs on the white throat
of a woman, jungle blood burning up, all are used by him to
tighten emotions almost to the breaking point.   No mock
heroics, no posturing, no theatricalism in Bancroft.   He is
Bull Weed and a magnificent animal, many magnificent animals
all in one.   Leonine, tigerish, rogue-elephantine, but animals
with the sublime gift of being able to grin.

Underworld does for the sophisticated adult what foot-
ball does for the college boy.   And Bancroft achieves some-
thing of the herculean glory of a gory fullback, with Von
Sternberg as his general, showing him the openings, guiding
his raging course.   Von Sternberg achieves impressionable
settings without the use of fancy photography.   At a gangster
ball Bull Weed wades knee-deep through paper ribbons to
rescue his girl from his enemy, and the confetti and the rib-
bons are like the sea, moving elementally all the while.   Von
Sternberg's genius lies in his ability to use for dramatic
effect shadows, lines, movement that naturally belong in the
picture.

For support Bancroft has two who catch the mood of

<u>Underworld</u> and who never slip therefrom, Clive Brook, gentleman-pal of Bull, and Evelyn Brent, feline mate of the jungle rogue. Both are better than they ever were before-- or may be again.

Nov. 14, 1927

The Jazz Singer

Heart throbs, tears, religion, "Mammy," love and syncopation--these made up The Jazz Singer as Al Jolson and the Vitaphone put over the vocal picture and the Warner Brothers' capital enterainment at the Garrick last evening.

Not a dry eye in the house when the jazz singer stood in the cantor's place in the synagogue and intoned the sacred hymns of his people, while his aged father within earshot lay dying, happy in the thought that his son, the fifth Rabinowitz, had not failed in his duty to the Lord.

It was gripping and tender and religious--just as was the play of the same title which ran here a year or so ago at the Harris, with still another gifted Jewish boy, George Jessel, playing the title role.

There is, of course, but one Jolson and he made the Jakie Rabinowitz, who ran away from his orthodox father's house and became a cabaret singer, a very real young man, the choice between duty and a career a difficult matter. The Vitaphone did a great deal to help, producing the songs and some of the other sounds in the course of the action.

Aside from the wonderful Jolson there are other fine actors in the cast. Warner Oland as Cantor Rabinowitz gives a notable characterization, as he usually does. Not enough has been said about the acting of this really cultured player. Oland has been an instructor of drama at Williams College and during that period translated the works of August Strindberg. His work in pictures has earned for him a high place.

Eugenie Besserer gives one of her inimitable impersonations, and May McAvoy is charming as always as the girl who takes an interest in the jazz singer and helps him along in his career.

The Garrick was crowded last night.   It is likely to be throughout the engagement with two performances daily.

Nov. 30, 1927